Put Money in Your Pocket

Vote to Double Your Income, Build the
Middle Class, and Make the 21st Century
an American Century

John Early

Copyright © 2017 & 2018 John H. Early

All rights reserved. No part of this publication may be reproduced, distributed, or transmitted in any form or by any means, including photocopying, recording, or other electronic or mechanical methods, without the prior written permission of the publisher, except in the case of brief quotations embodied in reviews and certain other non-commercial uses permitted by copyright law.

For Ellie Early and Jason Early

and parents everywhere who want their children and grandchildren to live in a prosperous nation.

Table of Contents

Introduction 9

Chapter 1 How *Not* to Run an Economy 15
    Real Economy vs. Money 15
    Getting Incentive Right 16
    The Most Important Price to Get Right 19
    What Drives the Price of Labor? 21
    The World as We See It 23

Chapter 2 The Key to Prosperity 27
    Marginal Tax Rate 28
    Only a Small Pocket for Workers 31
    The Big Tax-Free Pocket 32
    Top Marginal Rate and The Big Pocket 33
    Benefiting Workers and Business Owners 35

Chapter 3 The Dominant Influence on Growth 38
    Mental Disconnect 38
    History of the Top Rate and Growth 39
    The Top Bracket and Growth 44
    Capital-Gains Tax Rate and Growth 49
    How Many Tax Brackets? 52
    Corporate Income Tax 54
    The Model 56

Chapter 4 Restore the Value of Work 60

- Distributing Income Away from Workers...... 60
- Big Goals Require Work...... 62
- Wages and Marginal Tax Rate Connected...... 63
- The Tax-cut for the Wealthy that Helps Wages...... 64
- Capital Gains and Wages...... 66
- Wage Model...... 67
- Don't Blame Technology and Trade...... 68

Chapter 5 Stop Selling America Out to Other Nations...... 71
- Excessive Consumption: The Path to Downfall...... 71
- Tax Policy Explains Trade Deficit...... 74

Chapter 6 Our Place in the World...... 79
- Necessity of Treating Workers Well...... 80
- Over-Consuming Darkens Our Future...... 82

Chapter 7 Defusing the Budget Deficit Timebomb...... 86
- Revenue Growth...... 87
- Debt Expansion...... 91
- Trump Tax Cut Tees Up Crisis...... 92
- Solve It with Growth...... 94

Chapter 8 Bubbles and Real Capital...... 97
- Bubbles: It's Tax Policy, *NOT* Interest Rates...... 97
- Mal-Investment Bubbles...... 100
- Housing Bubble: A Symptom, *NOT* a Cause...... 102
- What is *Real* Capital?...... 103
- How to Avoid *Junk* Investment...... 105

Tax-cuts Killed Manufacturing Jobs 107

A Super Bubble? 109

Summary 113

Chapter 9 Paradigm Blindness 114

Trapped in the Box 115

Missing the Importance of Brackets 116

Theory at Odds with Reality 118

Tax Efficiency: The Wrong Goal 120

Bogus Laffer Curve 121

Staying in the Box 122

Chapter 10 Wolf in Sheep's Clothing Uses the Fed as a Scapegoat 125

Chapter 11 Hoover the Hero 135

Smoot Hawley Tariffs Didn't Cause Depression 135

Recovery Began with Hoover's Tax Increase 136

FDR: Best Tax Policy Ever 140

FDR's Attempt to Soak Rich Kills Economy 141

Economy Booms with Reagan Tax *Increase* 142

"Deal *(Crime)* of the Century" Ends Recession 144

Chapter 12 *Actual* "Pro-Growth" Tax Policy 145

A Deeper Look at Marginal Tax Rate's Impact on Growth 146

Tax-cuts for the 97% 155

Deeper Look into Capital Gains 158

Best Tax Schedule Ever 162

    Topping the Best Growth Ever? 165

    Use Genius Wisely 169

    Protecting the Big Pocket 171

    Tax Estates? 172

Chapter 13 Training Politicians.. 174

    We Voted for Crisis 175

    Stop Punishing the Good 178

Chapter 14 Looking Ahead 181

    GDP 183

    Wages 185

    Balance of Trade 186

    Learning the Lesson 187

Chapter 15 Crisis is Opportunity 190

    The Heartbeat of History 191

    We Are All In This Together 196

About the Author 203

Introduction

If you could vote for $9,200-a-year more income for yourself, would you do it? That would be a good start, but what if you could vote for the economy to *double* your income?

For that we need growth. The 1.7 percent rate the economy grew the last thirteen years won't cut it. We need to get growth up to the 4 or 5 percent range—or even better. Recent tax changes won't do that.

Now your personal decisions and actions will always have the biggest impact on your income—but why not let the national economy help you?

I'm not talking about what is called "Pro Growth" tax policy but is really a bait-and-switch that coddles elites and squeezes the middle class. Instead, I'll show you the tax policies which actually correspond with growth above 5 percent. These policies encourage everyone to work together to create widespread prosperity.

When enough of us vote for this, we won't have to worry about what happened to the work ethic or a low labor force participation rate—there will be more than enough incentive to work. When more people are working and producing more, asset prices are backed by real value rather than speculative fervor. So they won't drop 50 to 70 percent every few years when a recession comes.

Plus, when we learn to vote for prosperity it will eliminate the trade deficit. Bad tax policy has brought forty-two straight years of trade deficits which have taken almost twelve trillion dollars out of American's pockets while shifting ownership of US assets abroad. Taking care of our workers and maintaining our place in the world economy go hand in hand.

When we vote for prosperity, people will spend more money making the nation flourish and a lot less on politics trying to protect their interest in a stagnate or slowly growing pie. The middle class will grow again. We will have an attainable path to balance the federal budget in as little as eight years.

As people see that we are on the right track again, there will be a greater sense of community. We won't feel the need to call each other idiots for seeing things from a different perspective. With more economic security there will be less room for fear to incite hate between races and religions.

The solution requires learning the lesson we failed to learn from the Great Depression, the great recession, and the weak growth during and surrounding the 1990 recession. President Trump may be giving us another chance to learn the lesson. Until we learn it we can't solve the problem. We'll just react to symptoms. It's kind of like chasing a shadow into a dark room and blaming each other when we trip over things. Blaming the Fed, the rich or the poor, Mexico or China, regulations, or corrupt politicians only takes us deeper into the dark room.

This book shines the light you have been hoping for. Seeing it is simple, but not easy; you have been conditioned for decades to not see it. In the process, you may have to adjust a cherished belief or two, but this is vital for growth and prosperity.

The insights I will share with you come from over thirty years of searching for influences on the economy and financial markets. I prefer when the correlation between an influence and the actual result in the economy or market is huge, there is a sound, logical explanation for the relationship, and the influence gives a signal years ahead of time.

I always ask, When does the influence occur? If an indicator gives a signal and the economy tends to respond one year later, the indicator has a one-year lead time on the economy. I often calculate the strength of a correlation with several dozen different lead times before estimating the lead time most likely to correspond with changes in the economy or markets.

In 2006 I hit a bonanza analyzing how marginal tax rates influence economic growth. The correlations blew me away. The logic appeared rock-solid and the three indicators I was looking at had lead times on growth of two, three, and five years respectively. The lead times for influencing wages and jobs were even bigger.

The conclusions were the opposite of almost everything I had heard on the subject or learned in studying economics at Vanderbilt. I began to expect the worst recession in fifty years to start in 2007 or 2008.

On the evening of June 30, 2008 I was visiting with an economist from the Atlanta Fed while basking in a pleasant ocean breeze. The brisk activity in Honolulu only strengthened his view that the economy was robust and growing; it was a widely held belief. He didn't give much credence to my speculation that the recession had already started.

President George W. Bush, Treasury Secretary Hank Paulson, and Republican nominee John McCain were all still saying, "The economy is strong and fundamentally sound." A recent survey of the "Blue Chip Economists" showed about half thinking there was no chance of recession in the next two years—and the other half thought there was only a small chance of a downturn in the next two years.

We had come to the 83rd Annual Western Economic Association International (WEAI) Conference at the Sheraton Waikiki. In two days I was to present a paper in Session 180: "Growth Effects of Tax Policy on Ultra High Income." While over 200 people attended a few of the sessions, mine had about eleven—including my two children. The paper didn't make a big hit. It didn't fit into any of the models economists are trained to see through.

A few months later it was official: the great recession had begun January 2008.

The annual data points of the last eleven years strengthened the convictions reached in 2006.

Workers used to get about 50 percent of gross domestic product (GDP) in take-home pay. Now, it's around 43 percent.

That 7 percent difference amounts to about $9,200 for every worker in 2017.

Back when half the pie rewarded work, the economy grew faster and rewarded everyone. You paid heavily for the cost of uniformed voters—but we can fix it and you have a part to play.

By the end of Chapter 2 you will understand the influence marginal tax rates have on business owners, better than that of about 98 percent of the population (including most PhD economists). By the end of the book you will understand how to vote to solve our most pressing economic problems. You will no longer fall for the bait-and-switch that promises growth and more jobs, but actually delivers weakness and a concentration of wealth higher than the beneficial level.

Here's the crux of the book. We don't want the wealthy to pay more tax; we want them to build their wealth by taking less personal income, paying less tax, and plowing more of the revenue generated within businesses into growing their businesses or starting new ones. I call this "putting money in their big pocket." When our wealthy and talented have incentive to build and hold more of their wealth within a business, it creates prosperity for all.

But they won't do it unless we vote to give them the right incentive.

Americans intended to vote for prosperity, but we failed. The last thirty years grew at the slowest thirty year pace since the Great Depression. We got the policy we voted for, but not the results.

Will Trump's tax cut restore widespread, sustainable prosperity or is it a new wrinkle in the failed policy of the last 30 years? To understand this you will have to know when a tax policy influences growth. Otherwise, you are unable to recognize how the economic data is spun and become the puppet of the media and politicians.

If you don't know when the influence occurs you are likely to blame or credit current politicians for what previous ones did. You can't really even know what the economic news means.

To be part of the solution you need to understand the ideas in this book.

People with great economic power can rake in huge short-term gains from policies that harm their long-term economic well-being and may threaten the future of companies or even the country. When this happens, everyone else endures a lower standard of living in both the short- and long-term. Our only hope may be informed voters who don't fall for the slogans that hide reality and turn facts on their head.

Read on, my friends. Understanding and solutions lie in the pages ahead.

Chapter 1
How *Not* to Run an Economy

> *Money is like manure. If it piles up somewhere you get a stinkin' mess, but if you spread it around it makes things grow.* —Bunker Hunt

What makes an economy bad or good? What does an economy do? How will you distinguish class warfare from good policy? The quality of our future depends on understanding the answers to these questions. You will find the answers in this book, starting with this one: it is class *cooperation*, not warfare.

The height of economic mismanagement is when someone accumulates great wealth without benefiting society. Consider a hedge-fund manager who is clever enough to make a billion dollars in a year using the financial markets to take wealth away from others—then, to add insult to injury, gets most of the income taxed at the lower capital-gains tax rate.

Do you want the best and brightest among us focused on how to get any wealth you happen to create? Mismanagement runs rampant if we focus on the financial side of the economy in the short-term rather than the real economy in the long-term.

An *economy* is a system to satisfy the needs and wants of people. Every economic system has to answer some basic questions: What should be produced? How should it be made? And who gets to consume what is produced?

Real Economy vs. Money

If you think of the economy as a football game, the real economy is what goes on in the field of play. Money, like the scoreboard, is a measure of the game. When we watch the financial news, it's easy to think of the economy in dollar terms. Sure, we take the total dollar value of the economy and adjust by inflation to estimate the real economy. We tend to think the economy is still dollars—just inflation-adjusted ones—but it's not. It's not wages, it's hours of labor. It's not retail sales, it's manufacturing goods and distributing them. It's not profits, it's entrepreneurial zeal.

While much of the financial system supports making plays on the field, some people have figured out how to put scores on the board without contributing to the production of what actually benefits people. If unearned scores appeared on the board at a football game, it would be noticed and protested, perhaps even violently. In our complex economy scores on the board without plays on the field may go unnoticed or be praised in the financial media, but the effects are still felt and likely contribute to protesting and voting for change.

In the financial economy, we think of a secure retirement as having sufficient savings and investments like stocks, bonds, or money. The value of those financial assets is only as solid as the production of goods and services in the real economy.

The value of those claims—stocks, bonds, and so on—is highly dependent on the productivity of people who are in school while we are preparing for retirement. As we are busy saving for retirement, are students in schools learning to be productive? Will capitalists and entrepreneurs have the right incentive to employ them?

Getting Incentive Right

History makes clear the fact that a decentralized market economy takes better care of people than a centrally planned economy, but market economies have huge variations in how well they perform.

A well-run economy develops the potential of everyone's productivity and then gives them incentive to produce and benefit society. Incentive draws the most talented into creating the businesses and industries that enrich all of us. There is a social safety net that protects the ability to be productive when an individual goes through hard times, but does not encourage dependence. This safety net also acts as an automatic stabilizer to reduce the chance a recession becomes a self-perpetuating downward spiral.

Prices are the information system that transmits incentive through a market economy. The performance of the economy depends on the appropriateness of the price for goods, services, resources, capital, labor, and credit (interest rates).

In a well-run economy, the price of something represents the cost of production, a reasonable profit, and any social costs or benefits to society. If making a product creates pollution that harms individuals, the social cost of the harm is included in the price. If there is a benefit—if, for example, using recycled material in manufacturing actually benefits society—then the price would be lowered by that benefit.

When prices are right, markets beautifully allocate resources to maximize the well-being of all. Consumers don't have to understand environmental impact, fair labor practices, or anti-trust policy; they just need to shop wisely for value and let markets work their magic. To run the economy well, laws and regulations have the lightest touch possible that still brings the social costs or benefits into the price.

In a poorly run economy, developing potential is viewed as an expense. Many feel insecure in meeting basic needs. There is no social safety net, or it is ill-conceived and enables dependence or other destructive or non-productive behavior.

Regulations may be both lax, thus failing to protect people, and heavy-handed, unnecessarily driving up costs. They may serve to protect profits of large politically connected companies from new competition by driving up the costs for new entrants into the market place. Prices are wrong and the pursuit of profit may take advantage of workers or consumers. Those focused on profits may turn a blind eye to unsafe working conditions or pollution and risk accident, illness, or even death.

Concentration of wealth and income at the top is higher than the beneficial level needed to encourage our wealthy and talented to be productive. Or, at the other extreme, taxes are punitive and discourage those who have the most to contribute.

In a well-run economy, everyone's needs are amply met and the wildest dreams of many are fulfilled. In a poorly run economy, on the other hand, a few have great wealth and income while vast potential is left untapped; many struggle to meet basic needs and may only be one accident or illness away from great hardship.

In several ways, our economy is poorly run and President Donald Trump's campaign effectively tapped into the legitimate anxiety many have. If we think of the economy, gross domestic product (GDP), as one big pie produced each year, this book tries to answer the question, "What tax policy on personal income distributes the pie to encourage working together to make a bigger pie that can feed everyone?"

The opposite of that would be class *warfare*, which this book defines as a "shift in policy that changes how the pie is distributed, but does not contribute to faster growth of the pie." So if one class gets a change that gives them a bigger share, and the pie does not grow faster or perhaps grows slower or even shrinks, that is class warfare. If a change in policy shifts the distribution, but then the pie grows faster for everyone, we have not class warfare, but simply good policy.

Forget about distributing income. How do you distribute incentive to make the biggest, best pie possible? Doing what benefits all is a universal value. It's set out in the Constitution: "Promote the general welfare ..." It's the essence of Adam Smith's "invisible hand," where in well-run markets, advancing ones individual well-being is guided as if by an invisible hand to benefit everyone else. Jesus taught, "Love your neighbor as yourself."

How do we fairly divide the pie? The planet may have 7.5 billion different opinions. Measuring how much it grows has one measuring stick: GDP. We don't want to divide the pie evenly any more than we would want one person to eat the whole thing. We all benefit when those with great talent or resources get a bigger slice for creating bigger benefits for society. We all suffer when those with economic or political leverage take a bigger piece than they create, whether they are a CEO or a labor union. If someone takes too much, there is less incentive for others to contribute. "Why should I knock myself out to make somebody else rich?"

The Most Important Price to Get Right

Labor plays the biggest part in producing goods and services, and may be the most important price to get right. As I mentioned in the intro, about half the pie went to take-home pay in the 1950s, 1960s, and early 1970s. Figure 1-A shows the data. With this higher incentive to work and be productive, the economy annualized growing 3.9 percent during those twenty-five years. In the last forty-two years, the pie grew at 2.8 percent.

In the last thirteen years, where only 44 percent or less rewarded work, the economy only averaged 1.7 percent. In 2017, the 7 percent GDP difference between 43 percent and 50 percent was about 1.4

trillion dollars, or $9,200 per worker. If you add up the difference that didn't go to workers in the last forty-one years, it comes to about $21.8 trillion—and that's without adjusting for inflation!

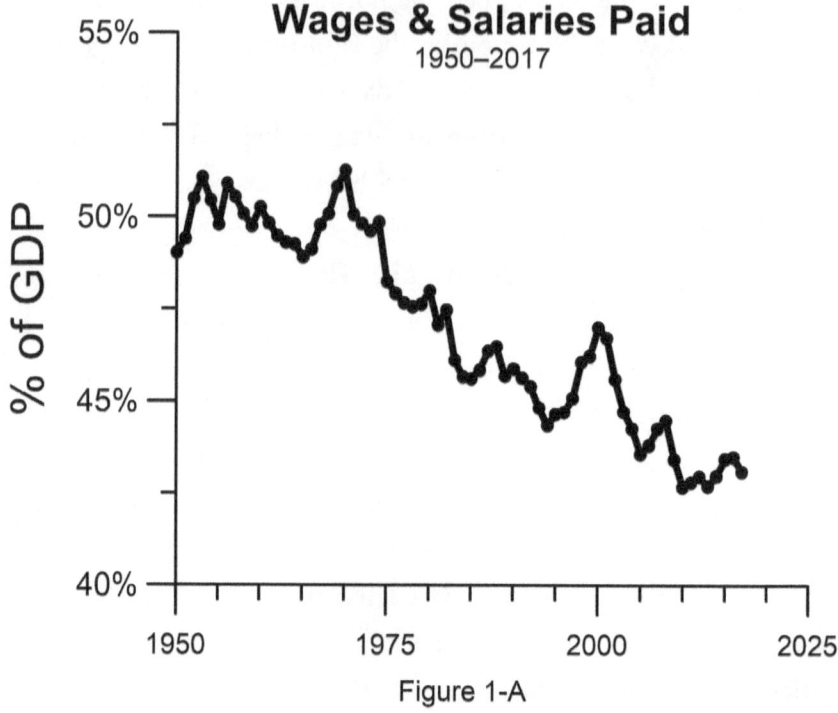

Figure 1-A

What if the larger share of the pie rewarding work was why the economy grew at 3.9 percent? If a 50 percent share and a 3.9 percent growth rate had continued the last forty-two years, the economy would be about 58 percent larger and workers would be getting about 84 percent more than they do today—and everyone else would be getting about 39 percent more. If 84 percent more and 39 percent more sound good, it is worth understanding what drives the long-term growth rate.

What Drives the Price of Labor?

The people who got that $21.8 trillion instead of it going to workers are quite content with the conventional explanation that labor's shrinking share is due to advancing technology, trade, and perhaps immigration depressing domestic wages. Or perhaps, people will believe the Federal Reserve is the culprit.

These explanations don't stand up to the data.

Technology does not explain the timing of the decline and certainly not the six-year advance in the 1990s while the Internet was growing at about 100 percent a year. Trade's explanation is doubtful; the North American Free Trade Agreement (NAFTA) went into effect before that six-year advance. We will cover this thoroughly in Chapter 4.

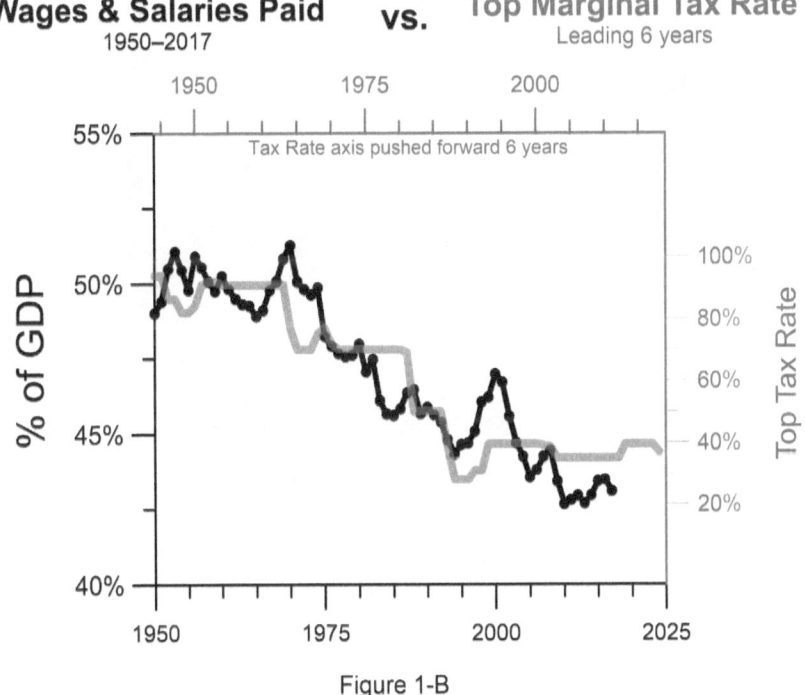

Figure 1-B

What if the decline in labor's share was instead influenced by the decline in the top marginal tax rate (as suggested in Figure 1-B)? This idea, that higher tax rates are better, sounds blasphemous to anyone steeped in the political and economic dialogue of the last fifty years.

Perhaps you can imagine dozens of reasons Figure 1-B is bogus. We could start with this: *correlation* does not mean *causation*. We could opine the six-year lead time shown is a totally implausible, arbitrary over-fitting of the data. As Nobel laureate Ronald Coase put it, "If you torture the data, it will confess."

If you are so doubtful, you probably also believe a low top marginal tax rate improves economic growth. Have you ever seen a chart with the top rate and growth rate together covering a long enough time span that it can't be cherry picked? Consider Figure 1-C.

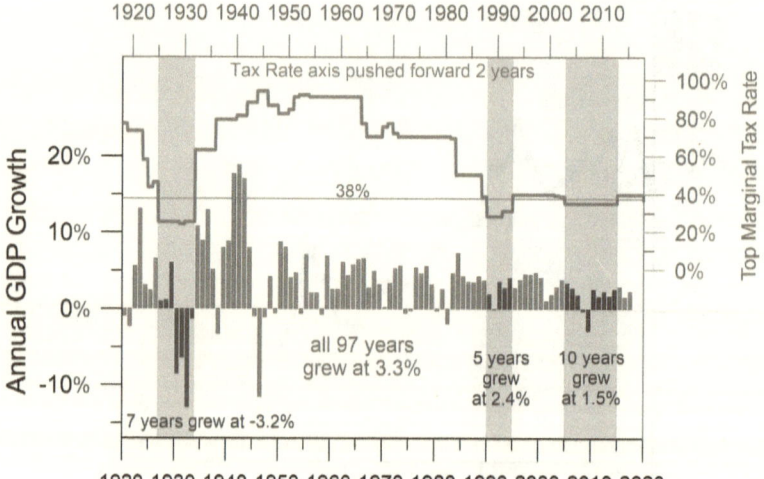

Shaded areas represent growth influenced by top rate below 38%.

22 years influenced by top tax rate <38% had average growth rate of **0.3%** using the **two year lead** time or **1.5%** with no lead time.

Figure 1-C

There are three periods where the top rate dropped below 38 percent in the last ninety-eight years; these are shaded in the chart. All three had below-average growth rates.

The introduction to this book mentioned that I often check dozens of lead times to find the strongest correlation. The top marginal tax rate has its strongest relationship to GDP growth with a two-year lead time. So, for example, the top tax rate of 35 percent in 2003 likely influenced growth in 2005 more than in any other year. The top rate was 35 percent from 2003 through 2012 and was one of the influences behind the 1.5 percent annual growth rate for GDP in the ten years from 2005 through 2014.

The 25 percent top rate in place for six of the seven years from 1925 through 1931, along with the 24 percent rate in 1929, correspond with the economy shrinking at an annualized rate of 3.2 percent for the seven years from 1927 through 1933. We will dig into the details of this in Chapter 3.

Cutting the top rate below 38 percent has no success stories in the U.S. in the last ninety-eight years, all three periods had below-average economic growth rates. Trump's cut to 37 percent in 2018 should start influencing growth in 2020. We should all pay close attention to what happens to growth in 2020 and beyond.

It's obvious in the chart there are other influences that lead to weak growth besides the top marginal rate being too low. The tax rate can also be too high.

The World as We See It

Given that we have been conditioned our whole lives to believe low tax rates are better, you likely doubt the accuracy of the chart. I encourage you to check the data yourself. I guarantee it is accurate.

We all experience the world through the filter of our conditioning. A few years back, I was running with Jack and Debbie near the edge of town, and there was another couple running the opposite direction. We crossed paths where a snake had been run over. The man passing by said three words. I heard "Flat head snake." Jack heard "Flat dead snake." Debbie heard "White head snake."

Whatever we happened to notice about the snake became a filter for interpreting the three words the man spoke. We don't see the world as it is, we see it as we are. We don't experience the world; we experience sensory inputs after they have been filtered through our past experience and current beliefs.

Filtering is why eye-witness testimony is often the least accurate evidence in a trial. The more ingrained the beliefs or the greater the perceived impact on one's believed source of livelihood or happiness, the stronger the filters.

Facts by themselves don't mean anything. It is the *context* of facts which determines meaning. Prior to the Civil War, both abolitionists and slaveholders used the same Bible verses to defend their positions. Republicans and Democrats can look at the same fact and reach opposite conclusions.

The fun and dangerous thing about opinions is that you don't have to know anything to have one. Being the social creatures we are, the views of our peers, group, tribe, religion, political party, race, or nationality usually have the greatest influence on our personal beliefs.

When someone claims a belief or opinion as "mine," identity gets entangled with the belief, and the person—myself included—may go to ridiculous lengths to defend the opinion. One reason Jesus says, "Blessed are the meek, for they shall inherit the earth" may be that the humble learn from experience faster because pride does not impel them to defend beliefs and positions shown to be false.

Communities and nations can be harmed or even brought to ruin from clinging to beliefs that have no basis in reality. Charles Mackay shares numerous examples of folly in his book, *Extraordinary Popular Delusions and the Madness of Crowds*. At the height of Tulip Mania in Holland, people would spend several years' worth of income on a single tulip bulb with the expectation of profit. Mackay says, "People go mad in herds and they only recover their senses slowly, and one by one."

Our divided nation could be on the verge of madness. The division feels familiar. I was raised in a mixed-up home. Did I say "mixed-up"? I meant *open minded*. My mother was a Republican, my father was a Democrat; they went to different churches; my father was raised with whippings; my mother was disciplined without physical punishment.

My father used to say, "My wife and I agree on everything except politics, religion, and how to raise children." Growing up, there were flush times where we were members of the country club, but also a few years where the budget required taking items back out of the grocery cart and an unexpected car repair was a near crisis. A paper route gave me the only money I had to spend.

Believing something yet knowing there was a different perspective that could be right was a part of growing up. While the division feels familiar, the acrimony between divisions does not. Both parents taught the value of compassion and respect for others.

Knowing there are always different viewpoints enabled me to find the concepts of this book. Conclusions from the data seemed overwhelming then, and the twelve annual data points since only strengthened the case. Yet, I have to step back and say, "This is how it *seems* to be" and be willing to see if new data supports or detracts from current conclusions.

Before you dismiss the implications of the last two charts, ask yourself: How well do you really understand marginal tax rates? Can you define what a "marginal tax rate" is? What is the difference between a marginal tax rate and the top marginal tax rate? How does an average tax rate differ from a marginal rate? How does the marginal rate influence a worker differently than it does a business owner? Most people cannot answer these questions.

So far we have shown important distinctions between the real economy and the financial one which help clarify what good economic policy is. We looked at the importance of incentives and prices. We defined *class warfare* and affirmed *benefiting all* is a universal principal. We have hinted getting the price of labor right and solving our economic growth problem relates to marginal tax rates. If the premise is correct, the first step to restoring widespread sustainable prosperity is to help you understand the answers to all those questions about marginal tax rates.

Turn the page, my friend, for understanding comes easy in the next chapter.

Chapter 2
The Key to Prosperity

In this chapter we explain the dominant influence behind prosperity and show the context in which it works. Marginal tax rates drive this influence, but since almost no one understands marginal rates, we will explain them with concrete examples and then show how they influence workers and business owners.

The cause of something is always multifaceted; it may depend on thousands of favorable conditions, necessary pre-conditions, and one or more triggers or catalysts. In this book we are narrowing the context of the key to long-term prosperity in the United States over the last ninety-seven years.

Incentive matters. If we want our wealthy and talented to create businesses and industries that create prosperity for everyone, they need to be well rewarded. The key to prosperity has two parts: the incentive to *run* businesses and the incentive to *grow* them.

The first part requires an expected favorable combination of after-tax income and the future value of the business. The second part encourages business owners to focus more on growing their businesses. We will call after-tax income the "small pocket" and the value of their businesses the "big pocket."

The more owners put into growing the business, the faster their big pocket and the economy grow. Marginal tax rates influence whether money goes in the big pocket or the small pocket—but, as has been said, almost no one understands marginal tax rates.

Marginal Tax Rate

The marginal tax rate is the tax paid on an additional dollar of income—or on the *last* dollar of income. Understanding them takes more than knowing this definition.

David Norris was the number-two person at Happy State Bank and an integral part of growing the bank from being the 812th biggest bank in Texas (out of about 875) in 1990 to the 18th largest (out of 660) in 2014. He is now using the tools and insights in achievement to help people get past the limitations they create for themselves and fulfill their dreams. He is a speaker, trainer, and coach at DavidNorrisLeadership.com. He calls it "Selling tickets to his world."

David didn't understand marginal tax rates until he watched a three-minute video I produced, How to Vote for Prosperity in 3 Minutes. Before that, he'd just sent his information to the accountant and paid whatever the tax was. After the video, he realized he had great discretion on how much income to take from the business. He could take more income and owe more tax or take less income and owe less tax. Now he takes less income, pays less tax, and plows more of the revenue into deductible expenditures that grow the value of his business. He thinks of it as putting money in his pocket—his "big pocket."

A couple I talked with several years ago shared the misconception that most people have. She was a teacher and he was an engineer. She had prepared their annual tax return for years and was sure she understood how marginal taxes worked. They were in the 28 percent bracket, so their marginal tax rate was 28 percent. She adamantly insisted they paid 28 percent of their income in Federal income tax.

If you share this misunderstanding, it might be a good exercise to get out your tax return and find the amount of tax paid, then divide it by your adjusted gross income. This will give your average tax rate, and you'll find it is substantially lower than your marginal tax rate. Surprised? Don't worry. Doing this years ago was a pleasant surprise for me.

A simple example of a single woman without children with all-wage income can help us understand. She would use the standard deduction (which in 2018 is $12,200) so her first $12,200 of income is tax-free. So the average rate and marginal are both zero percent through $12,200. Income above that point becomes taxable income. On the next dollar of income, the marginal rate jumps to 10 percent.

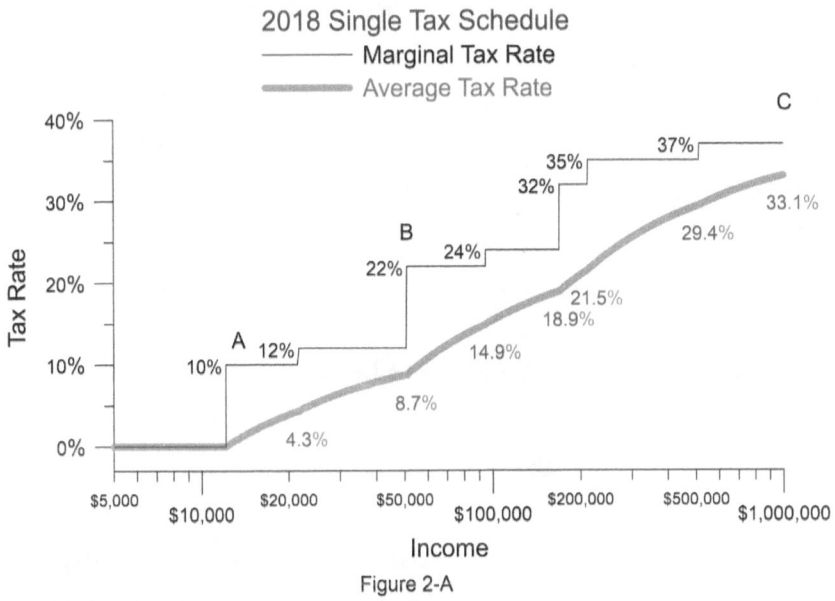

Figure 2-A

If she had a $1,000 dollars of taxable income or $13,200 of total income (point A on Figure 2-A), she would owe $100 in income tax at her marginal rate of 10 percent. This $100 would be 0.8 percent of her income. If she had $50,900 of income (point B) she would pay zero percent on the first $12,200, 10 percent on the next $9,525, and 12 percent on the rest of the $59,000. Her average rate would be

8.7 percent and her marginal rate on the last dollar would be that 12 percent. If she earned one more dollar, the marginal rate on that dollar would jump to 22 percent. If she had a million-dollar income (point C) her average rate would be 33.1 percent and her marginal rate would be the *top* marginal rate of 37 percent.

In Figure 2-A, it was easier to display the effect of brackets using a logarithmic scale for income. You may notice the distance on the scale going from $10,000 to $100,000 is the same as going from $100,000 to a million.

A married couple with a $5 million income might have $200,000 of itemized deductions, so they would use itemized deductions rather than the standard deduction. Taxable income for them would not start until $200,000. They would also likely have significant long-term capital gains and qualified dividend income, which has its own schedule of tax brackets topping out at 20 percent or 23.8 percent with the Medicare surtax.

A capital gain is *the increase in the value of an asset at the time of sell*. So if you bought shares of stock or a whole business for $100,000 and sold it years later for $250,000, you would have a $150,000 capital gain. The gain would be taxed at the lower capital-gains tax rate. Ideally, the lower capital-gain tax rate encourages growing businesses and the economy over the long-term.

Income from a business organized as a sole proprietorship, a partnership, or an S corporation *passes through* to the owner(s) as personal income. For example, the Trump family has over 500 businesses that generate pass-through income. The tax cut gives up to a 20 percent discount on pass-through income. So in effect the top marginal tax rate on such personal income could be 29.6 percent instead of 37 percent.

However, the tax change adds a significant layer of complexity for business owners trying to figure out their marginal tax rate. The

20 percent discount starts phasing out as incomes get larger unless the business has a sufficient combination of capital and or wage and salary expense.

The uncertainty for 2018 is higher because the precise rules governing the discount have not yet been written by the IRS. Some of the rules probably won't be final until court cases settle them.

Only a Small Pocket for Workers

Despite the complexity of the discount on pass-through income you should have a clearer understanding of marginal tax rates and brackets, so now we can talk about how tax rates affect the money going into people's pockets. Workers just have a small pocket, and marginal tax rates make working less attractive. The higher the marginal tax rate, the less incentive to work.

President Ronald Reagan was an actor in 1944 and '45, when the top rate was 94 percent on income above $200,000. He would make one film a year, hit the top rate of 94 percent, and take the rest of the year off. He saw no point in working to keep only 6 percent of his earnings.

This is an example of what N. Gregory Mankiw, Matthew Weinzierl, and Danny Yagan describe in their article "Optimal Taxation in Theory and Practice" in *The Journal of Economic Perspectives*. The article showed people were less willing to work with higher marginal tax rates; or, as an economist would describe it, the supply of labor goes *down* when marginal tax rates go *up*.

They found this effect most prevalent on income up to about two and a half times the median wage. If correct, economic growth and the supply of labor benefit by having low marginal tax rates on income below about $140,000. The Trump tax cut improved this incentive to work and should help growth some, but this change will not unclog the growth engine. We must change the incentive for business owners.

The Big Tax-Free Pocket

Business owners have the same "small pocket" that workers do, and are thus just as eager for personal income tax rates to be cut. However, business owners also have the "big pocket" with the value of their business. Owners have great discretion on which pocket to put money in. When the wealthy and talented decide whether or not to run a business, they look at both pockets: the after-tax income in the small pocket and expected growth in value in the big pocket. The deductible or depreciable expenditures that grow their big pocket reduce taxable income in their small pocket. This is true for sole proprietors and for publicly traded companies deciding to pay dividends or upgrade equipment.

When you run a business, how much tax you pay—or even if you pay tax at all—is optional. When an entrepreneur spends business revenue, or income from any source, on wages, marketing, equipment, research, or training, those dollars are not taxed. When those expenditures grow the value of the business, the increased value of the business is not taxed. If the business is sold, it could be taxed at the lower capital-gains rate.

In estate planning, if the owner passing on will not diminish the value of the business, the capital-gains tax can be avoided. In an estate, assets such as a business get a stepped-up cost basis, so there is no longer a capital gain to be taxed. If the owner's estate, including the value of the business, is less than $11.2 million, no estate tax is due. If the owner is married, the estate tax exemption doubles to almost $22.4 million. If the value of the business has grown to $500 million and the owner doesn't want to pay estate taxes, he could set up a charitable foundation with $477.6 million and not pay any estate taxes. If the couple wanted, the children could run the foundation and draw a salary as they oversaw giving money to worthy causes.

The other way to not pay any estate tax on a $500-million estate is to spend enough money electing politicians who will eliminate the estate tax. This happened briefly in 2010. Long time Washington politicians are usually sympathetic to cutting/eliminating the estate tax as they often have generated enough wealth to pay it.

Top Marginal Rate and The Big Pocket

You only pay income tax on the money you put in the small pocket. Dollars spent growing the business can remain tax-free forever.

Marginal tax rates affect business owners differently than workers because of the big pocket. The higher the marginal tax rate is on the small pocket, the more attractive putting money in the big tax-free pocket becomes.

When more money goes in the big pocket, more gets spent on wages, marketing, research, equipment, and so on. Collectively, the more money business owners put in the big pocket the faster their businesses and the economy grows. Conversely, if the marginal tax rate is too low the big pocket gets less attention and lots of money flows into the small pocket. We saw this in the last chapter where Figure 1-C showed a top rate below 38 percent corresponded with weak growth.

The slogan "If we cut taxes, businesses will have more money to hire people and grow the economy" totally misses how the big pocket works. Political rhetoric, financial media, and economic literature all fail to recognize the existence of the big pocket when they talk about marginal tax rates.

But accountants get it.

My first job out of college was in sales at Micro Mike's, Incorporated. My family had bought computers from this company and had also invested in it. One of their customers, Curtis Sales, had one of the best selections of pickup truck accessories in the country. They were having a very good 1982. The top marginal tax rate was 50 percent, and their accountant told them they needed to buy some equipment or they were going to pay too much in taxes. They bought a new multiuser point-of-sale system.

While this wasn't my sale, I still had a part in it. About a year earlier I'd invested $10,000 in the company; they took the money and bought a five-megabyte hard drive designed for a mainframe computer. It was about as big and as loud as a lawnmower. They were the first company to code a disk operating system to put a hard drive on a microcomputer.

In just a few months, they had the lead on the technology and could do things with a microcomputer that previously took a vastly more expensive mainframe or minicomputer; they shot to a million dollars in sales. Their multiuser system depended on the hard drive. When I joined the company, they were on their way to being displaced by the IBM PC. When I left to work in the family office, I thought they would go under in a month. They lasted another year.

High-income business people understand the big pocket when they face high marginal rates, but when they tell you what kind of tax rate they want, they are thinking about the small pocket. During summers in grade school, my grandmother would sometimes take me to the board room of the Globe News. She and many of her twelve brothers and sisters would often gather there. They owned the majority interest of the newspaper, a television station and a radio station in Amarillo, Texas.

They were all grandchildren of J. A. Whittenberg, who ran away from home in Missouri on his twelfth birthday in 1869 with twelve dollars to find an older brother in Texas. He learned the cattle business and loved it. He and his wife saved and invested in land and cattle together. In Hutchinson County where they finally settled, land was selling for fifty cents to five dollars an acre. They accumulated 32,000 acres. It turned out a vast oil dome extended under much of the land. By 1926 they had a net worth around $30 million.

I was sitting in the board room, in about 1968, listening to my great-uncle Roy Whittenberg encourage his siblings to invest in an oil well. The top tax rate then was 75.25 percent. From the conversation, I remember the context suggested all or most of them were in that top bracket.

Roy was saying something like, "There really is no reason not to invest. Even if the well turns out to be a dry hole, you'll be able to save seventy-five percent of the cost on taxes. If it hits, you'll be able to deduct a lot of the cost right away from taxes and there will probably be more wells nearby to drill with more deductions and it could provide income for decades to you and your children and grandchildren." The high tax rate was a big selling point to making the deductible investment.

Benefiting Workers and Business Owners

While workers and business owners are influenced differently by marginal tax rates, there is some common interest that benefits growth: low marginal rates for income below about $140,000 will both encourage more work and make the small-pocket side of running a business more attractive.

In Chapter 3, we'll see another way to help growth with tax-cuts for the wealthy: raise the tax brackets. If in the example of our single tax payer we raised all the brackets 20 percent, taxable income would begin at $14,600 rather than at $12,200. The average tax rate on a $150,000 income would drop from 18.3 to 17.1 percent, saving about $1,700, while the marginal rate would remain at 24 percent. This is shown as point A on Figure 2-B. Raising brackets increases the small-pocket incentive for employees to work more. It also increases the small-pocket incentive to run a business while preserving the influence of marginal tax rates to grow businesses.

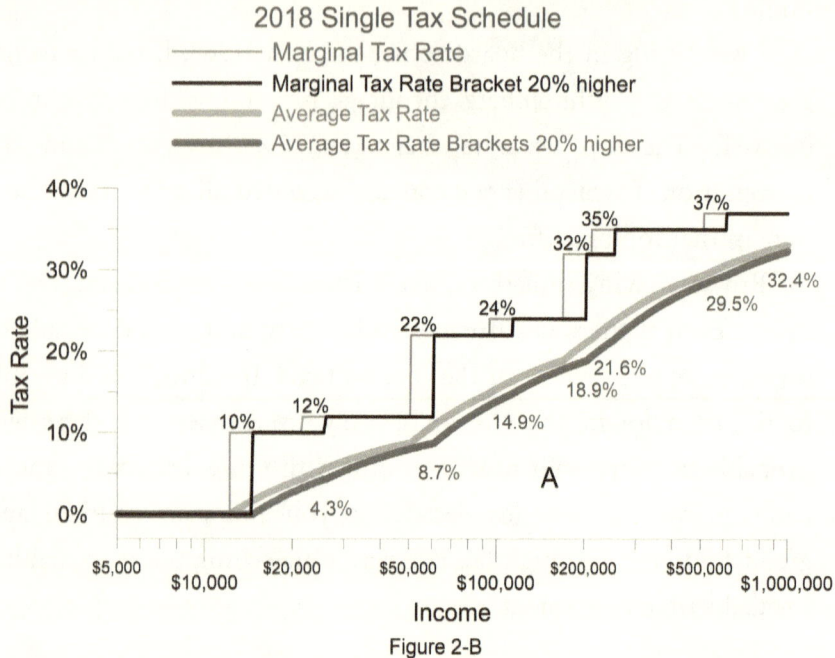

Figure 2-B

In Chapter 4, we'll see how raising brackets benefits workers beyond just the increase in after-tax income.

At this point you have taken the first step to restoring prosperity by understanding how marginal tax rates work. You probably now understand them as well as almost anyone in the world. You know that once income becomes large enough to include taxable income, the average tax rate is always lower than the marginal rate. You know how brackets work. You probably already understood how marginal tax rates affect workers, but now you're an expert on the subject.

Now you understand business owners have what we are calling a "small pocket" and a "big pocket" and that they can avoid taxes by putting money in the big pocket and growing their businesses. You understand the marginal tax rate influences whether a business owner is better off putting money in the big pocket or the small pocket.

You have seen a theoretical possibility that a high marginal tax rate could encourage growing a business and the economy. You are now set up to take the second step. This is where you adjust your view of what makes the economy strong to bring it more in line with the historical reality.

The second step begins in Chapter 3, where we dig into the data to show how marginal tax rates can encourage growth. It may take the rest of the book, or it may take that plus observing the next seven years of growth from this new perspective. For those that take the second step, the third step will be easy and clear. You vote for strength and prosperity in every national election.

Chapter 3
The Dominant Influence on Growth

You are about to get valuable context to help understand the likely impact of Trump's tax changes as well as the tax policy for the last ninety-eight years. We will take a little walk down the path that led to conclusions in 2006 and include the more recent data that supports those conclusions.

We will examine the influence the top marginal tax rate has on growth and also the impact of the capital-gains tax rate. These two tax rates appear to be Goldilocks variables—where you don't want them too high or too low, but just right.

To understand those influences, the path needs a twist to examine the top bracket. Turns out the top bracket, in addition to influencing growth, also impacts where the Goldilocks points are for the top rate and the capital-gain rate. We will also look at the number of brackets and the top corporate income tax rate. Then we'll show a model made with the data that forecasts growth a couple years into the future.

Mental Disconnect

This journey to understand tax policy began in 2006 with a growing mental disconnect between what I had been observing in the data and everything I had been taught and conditioned to believe about tax policy and growth. I follow the release of economic data, such as jobs or GDP, kind of like watching to see if the Dallas Cowboys will score a touchdown. Except with economic data it's like knowing all the touchdowns, field goals, and fumbles for the last 100 years—or at least having quick access in a handy database and being able to quickly compare the current situation to the past.

Prior to 2000, the economy usually grew at 4 percent or better during an expansion and would shrink enough during a recession to pull the long-term growth rate down to about 3.5 percent. The first four years of this expansion, 2002-2005, had annualized less than 3 percent.

The peak year, 2004, at 3.8 percent, was weak compared to previous expansions. The best year under Carter was 5.6 percent; Reagan had a 7.3 percent year; Clinton's best year was 4.7 percent. I also kept remembering what Newt Gingrich said in debate against the 1993 tax increase, "You can't raise taxes. It will cause a recession." Yet, taxes *were* raised, and instead of a recession the expansion lasted almost eight more years. It was the longest expansion ever. And still is.

History of the Top Rate and Growth

I didn't have the history of the top tax rate in the data base, so I went and found it. The data went back to 1913, when the income tax began. The U.S. Department of Commerce: Bureau of Economic Analysis has annual GDP data back to 1929. I also wanted to know the growth rates that preceded The Great Depression. There are some databases and books with GDP data going back into the nineteenth century. All GDP data is an estimate of the production of goods and services. Occasionally, better ways to make those estimates are found and the Bureau of Economic Analysis will tweak historical GDP data. Data prior to 1929 does not get updated; it is probably less accurate, but still useful.

So, just to warn you, we are about to get into lots of data and charts. Some of you will find them tedious. If you want to skip over the charts and their descriptions it's okay. You can still understand the ideas and conclusions without them. If you want to see this from a slightly different perspective with color charts, you can watch Tax Policy for Prosperity, a nine-minute YouTube video I made.

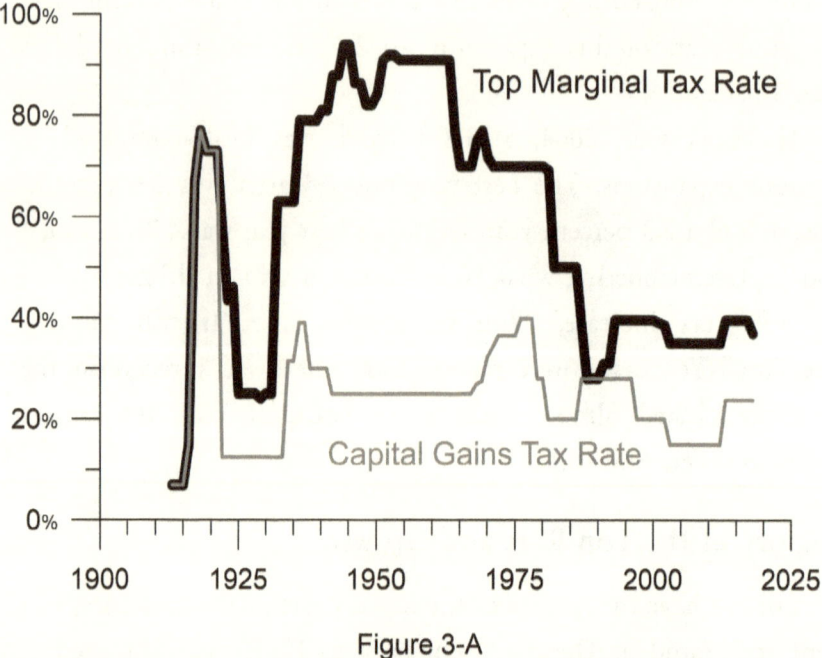

Figure 3-A

You may have already figured out I am going to recommend higher marginal tax rates at high incomes. Hopefully you have not jumped to the conclusion that I'm advocating bigger government. The size of government is a separate issue from the progressivity of the tax code.

For example, while the top tax rate was 79 percent from 1936 to 1939, Federal revenue averaged less than 7 percent of GDP compared with about 19 percent today. So the Federal government took in about a third of the share of GDP in revenue with a top marginal rate that was more than twice as high as it is today.

The impact of tax policy on growth shown below is pretty clear to me. The influence on growth from the size of government, however, is not clear to me, and this book does not take a position on government being smaller or bigger.

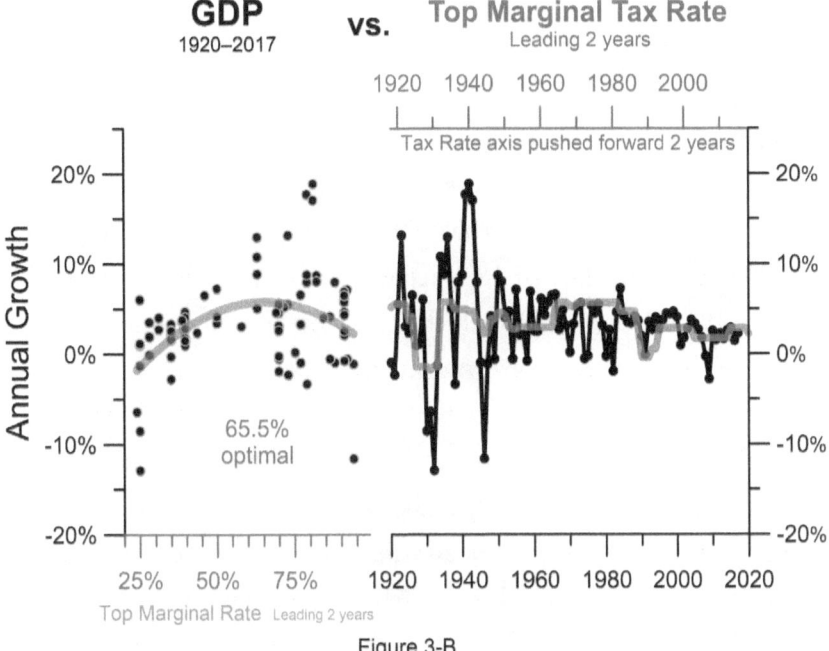

Figure 3-B

The first stab at understanding the relationship between the top tax rate and growth was a scatter plot similar to the left side of Figure 3-B. A scatter plot is a graph in which the values of two variables are plotted along two axes; the pattern of the resulting points reveals any correlation present. If you already understand how scatter-plot and time-series charts work, you can skip the next four paragraphs.

There is a lot going on with this chart. You may want to take a little time to understand its data. When you do, you will understand all the charts in this book. We'll take it step-by-step. The two sides of this chart show the same data in different formats. The left side is a scatter plot; the right side, a time-series. The black vertical y-axes on the left and the right are mirror images of each other and show the annual GDP growth rate. The GDP growth rate is the black line with the dots on the right side. You saw this growth data in Figure 1-C, but it was plotted as a bar chart rather than as a line. As in figure 1-C, the gray time-scale axis for the tax rate is pushed forward to show the two-year lead time.

The scatter plot on the left uses the black annual-growth axis and the gray top marginal tax-rate axis with a two-year lead time. Each dot, or point, represents the growth rate for a year and the top tax rate that influenced the growth. For example, the highest point shows 1942's growth rate of 18.9 percent and the 81 percent top tax rate from 1940. Remember: with the two-year lead time, the top tax rate in 1940 influences the growth rate in 1942.

The curved gray line on the scatter plot is the quadratic equation of the tax rate and growth rate which have the best fit with all the dots. Usually I will call this the "curvilinear best-fit line."

The high point in this quadratic equation comes at a 65.5 percent marginal tax rate. This is what we were talking about with the Goldilocks top tax rate: not too high, not too low, but just right. The equation estimates a 5.8 percent growth with a 65.5 percent top rate.

Each dot on the scatter plot has a corresponding dot on the black growth-rate line in the time-series chart on the right. Likewise, the gray line on the time-series chart corresponds to the best curvilinear fit from the scatter plot. I take this quadratic equation and plug in the top marginal rate to estimate a GDP growth rate. These estimates are the gray line. For example, the 24 percent top rate from 1929 calculates as a minus-1.8 percent growth estimate for 1931. This is the lowest point for the gray line on both sides of the chart.

Since there is a two-year lead time, the top rate of 39.6 percent in 2015, '16 and '17 estimates growth of 2.8 percent for 2017, 18 and '19. Changing the top rate in 2018 should start influencing growth in 2020.

"Lead time" and a curvilinear fit are areas in which I may be adding to economic thought. I have examined numerous academic papers about taxes and growth in economic journals; none that I have found say when the tax rate is supposed to influence growth, or specified that they examined a curvilinear fit.

The papers that examine the empirical correlation between growth and taxes usually conclude there is no significant relationship between growth and the marginal tax rate. They appear to only examine a linear correlation and miss the more significant curvilinear relationship. They do not say multiple lead times were examined or claim one lead time had more influence than another. The theoretical papers which usually hypothesize low marginal rates improve growth also say nothing about when the influence should occur.

To pick the best lead time, I compared the strength of the correlation of the best-fit line with points in the scatter plot. I examined the correlation with lead times ranging from the top rate lagging growth one year all the way out to the top tax rate leading eight years. The correlations with the tax rate lagging one year and on a concurrent basis were too weak to be meaningful. With the top rate leading a year, the correlation began to be meaningful. The correlation peaked with a two-year lead and then got progressively weaker as the lead time increased.

When I first created a chart like this it looked significant and the statistical test of the relationship supported the view, but correlation was not really all that strong. If you have had a college course in statistics, you have probably heard of the correlation measure called R-squared. This is a statistical measure of how close the data is to a fitted line; it is sometimes referred to as the "coefficient of determination"; it varies from 1 to 0. If you haven't heard of this before, just remember: "1" is a perfect correlation where all the dots would be on the best-fit line, and "0" has no correlation where the dots would be in a random cloud around a flat horizontal line. The R-squared for the chart is 0.18, which implies 18 percent of the variation in annual growth is influenced by the top tax rate from two years earlier.

In studying the chart, I began to wonder what could explain some of the big gaps between actual GDP growth and the estimate using the top rate. There was the obvious miss where the WWII years had much stronger growth than the estimate. I was a bit more perplexed with a period I had lived through from 1967 to 1982 where the gray line suggested the 70 percent top rate would lead to 5.7 percent growth. The period actually grew at 2.7 percent, and every year was weaker than the estimate.

The Top Bracket and Growth

The webpage where I found the top tax rate data also had the top bracket data. Since I already had that data, I thought it couldn't hurt to check it out, and, sure enough, there was a big reward for my analysis.

Making the plot of the bracket meaningful when the data varies from millions down to $28,000 is easier using a logarithmic, or log scale. We talked a bit about this in Chapter 2, that a percentage change is the same anywhere on the scale, so doubling from 1 to 2 is the same distance on the scale as doubling from 4,000 to 8,000.

In addition to making sense of a big data range, a constant growth rate can be plotted on a log scale as a straight line. On a linear scale, a constant rate of growth plots as a parabolic curve.

I was kind of shocked when I saw that the top bracket had been $5 million from 1936 to 1941. Adjusted for inflation, this would be

$88 million today. After working with the data, I found adjusting the bracket by multiples of the previous year's GDP per person (GDP/p) had a better correlation to growth than adjusting for inflation.

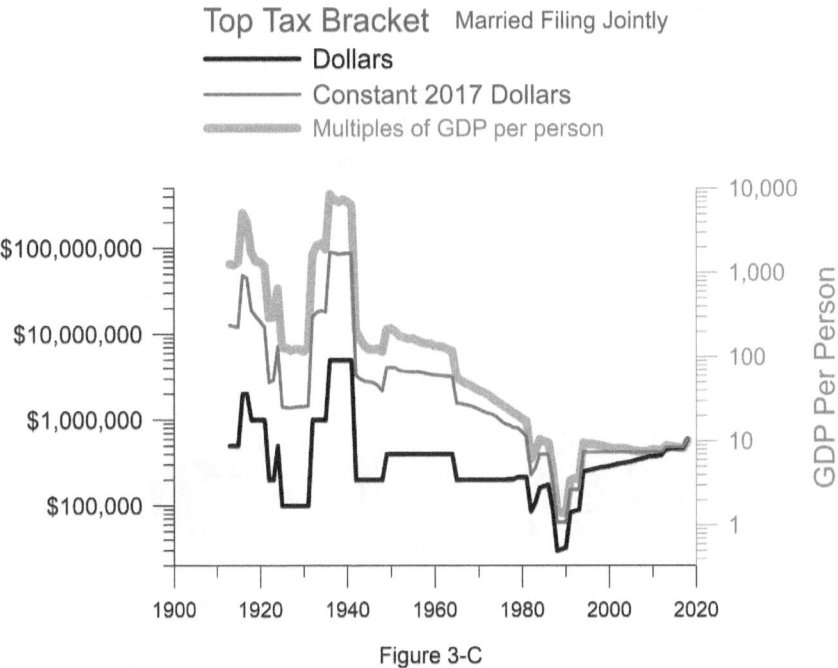

Figure 3-C

In 1936, the $5-million bracket was 8,571 GDP/p. That would be equivalent to $510 million in 2018. By contrast, the top bracket in 2017 was 8.2 GDP/p. Trump's tax cut raised the top bracket to $600,000 or 10.1 GDP/p. In GDP/p terms this is the highest bracket since 1981, but the bracket has been eight hundred and fifty times higher. In dollar terms it's the highest since 1941.

Growth tends to get better as the top bracket goes up. Higher brackets make it easier to put enough after tax money in business owners' small pockets to encourage running a business while having high enough marginal rates to encourage growing a business. When a high marginal rate only applies to a very high level of income, the small-pocket incentive and big-pocket incentive can work in harmony to encourage prosperity.

Raising the bracket to $600,000 is a good step, but to have a meaningful impact on growth the dollar level needs to go to the tens or hundreds of millions.

The top bracket has its strongest relationship to GDP with a three-year lead time. The gray line in Figure 3-D is a power fit.

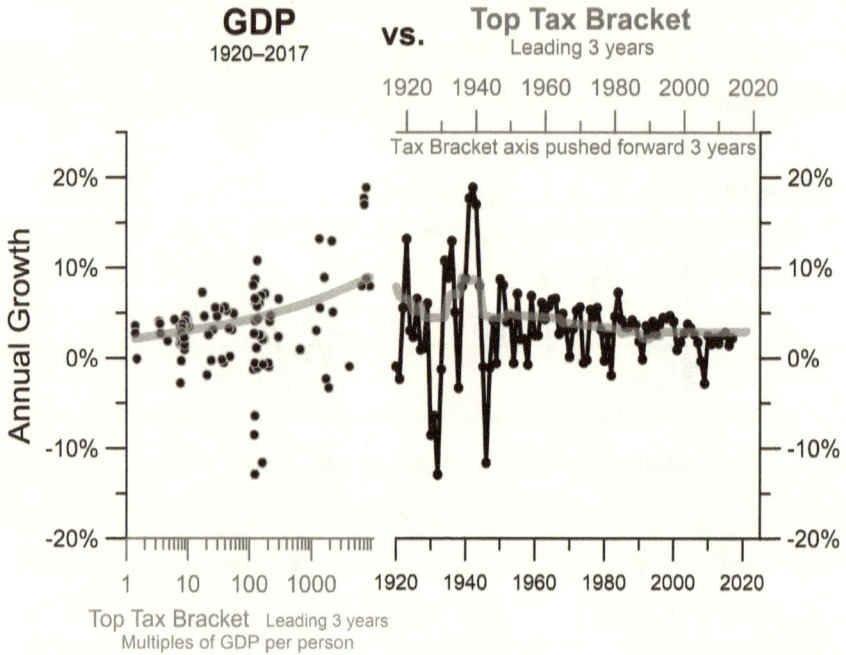

Figure 3-D

A watershed moment of sorts came in 1965 when the top bracket was cut from $400,000 to $200,000. Prior to that, the top bracket had never been less than 115 GDP/p. Since then it has never been more than 56 GDP/p. For our purposes, we define the pre-1965 period as the "High Bracket era" and 1965 and after as the "Low Bracket era." Using these two eras allows more accurate and useful correlations between GDP and the top tax rate.

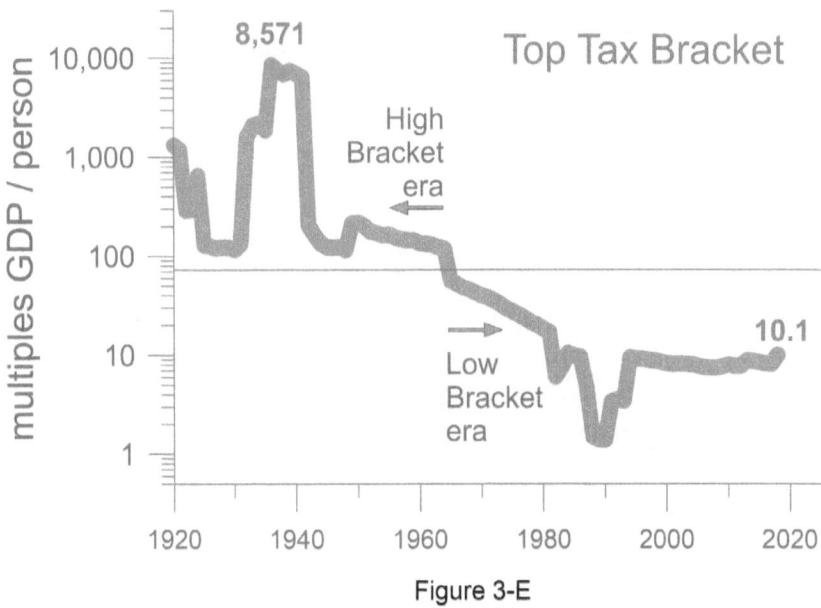

Figure 3-E

In the Low Bracket era Figure 3-F, the best-fit curve suggests a 54.5 percent top rate maximizes growth. A 50 percent top rate is the closest we got to the implied optimal, however, and that was the rate influencing the 7.3 percent growth in 1984. This is the high point on the chart. The weakest growth influenced by the 50 percent top rate was 3.5 percent in 1987.

The Great Recession and financial crisis was influenced by the too-low 35 percent top rate. The 1990 recession and weak growth before and after were influenced by the too-low 28 percent top rate. This chart clears up the puzzle about the 70 percent top rate having low growth in Figure 3-B. A top bracket less than 56 GDP/p is way too low for a top tax rate of 70 percent, and harms the incentive needed for the small pocket.

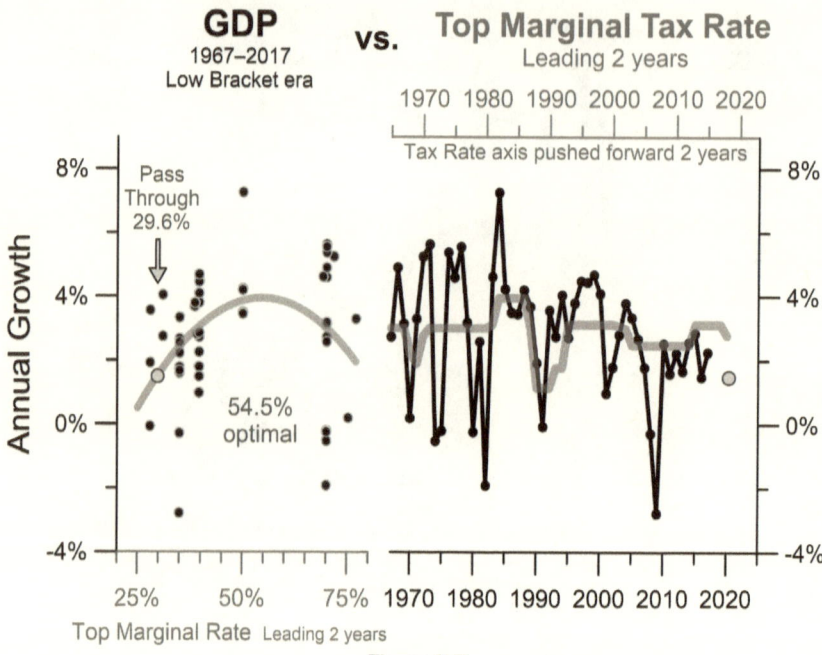

Figure 3-F

At the other extreme, the too-high top rate of 75.25 percent in 1968 corresponds with a recession in 1970.

Trump's top rate of 37 percent would imply 2.8 percent growth. However, the tax rate that influences how much revenue elite business owners pull out as income will likely be the pass-through rate which might be as low as 29.6 percent which implies growth at 1.5 percent. This is represented as a gray dot with a black circle around it on both sides of Figure 3-F.

Best-fit curve in the High Bracket era shown in Figure 3-G suggests 64 percent would optimize growth. The three years influenced by the 63 percent top rate, 1934–'36, annualized growing almost 11 percent. The 25 percent top rate was far below the optimal and corresponds with the Great Depression; the too-high 94 percent rate also had terrible results. The best growth actually was influenced by the 81 percent top tax rate; however, this was also influenced by the top bracket, as shown in Figure 3-D, by WWII and by the capital-gains rate which we cover next.

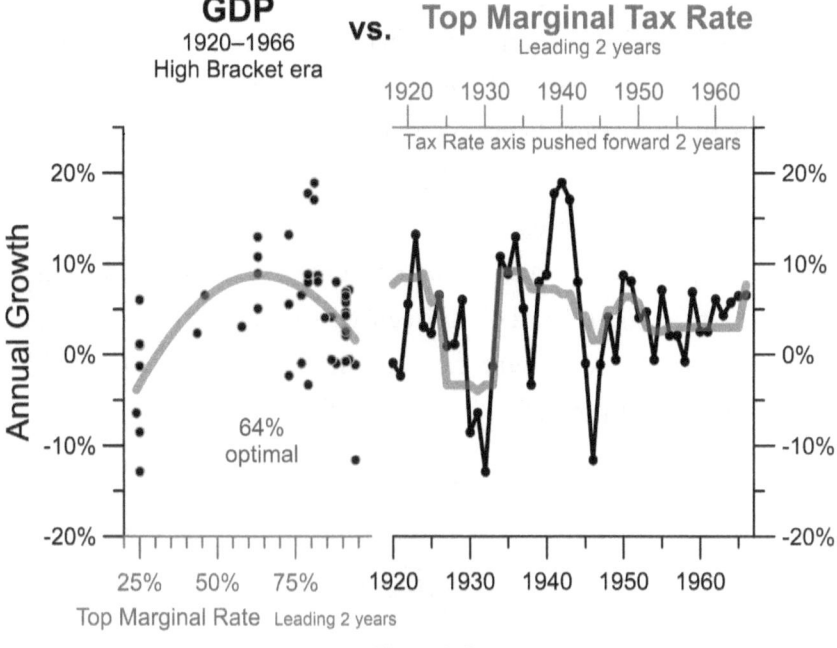

Figure 3-G

Capital-Gains Tax Rate and Growth

Capital gains also has a schedule of marginal tax brackets: its schedule has lower tax rates than the schedule for ordinary income. When people talk about the capital-gains tax rate, they generally refer to the tax rate at the top bracket for long-term capital gains. Unless otherwise stated, the capital-gains tax rate will refer to the rate at its top bracket.

To get the lower long-term capital-gains tax rate, you have to own the asset for a designated time period (currently one year; the holding period to get the biggest discount has been as long as ten years). Ideally, the lower tax rate on capital gains encourages investments with longer-term benefits to society. It's about growing assets. The capital-gains tax rate applies to assets that are not your business. So an individual could sell a car for more than she paid and count it as a capital gain, but a car dealership could not.

The capital-gains tax rate has its biggest influence on growth with a five-year lead time—although, in the Low Bracket era, there is a case for the lead time being four years. Figure 3-H uses the five-year lead. A 29 percent capital-gains rate appears to maximize growth in the Low Bracket era. The closest we got to this optimal rate was 28 percent for two years from 1979-'80 and for ten years from 1987 through 1996. This influenced growth in 1984-'85 and 1992-2001. So the 28 percent capital-gains rate influenced the 7.3 percent GDP growth in 1984 and all the Clinton years.

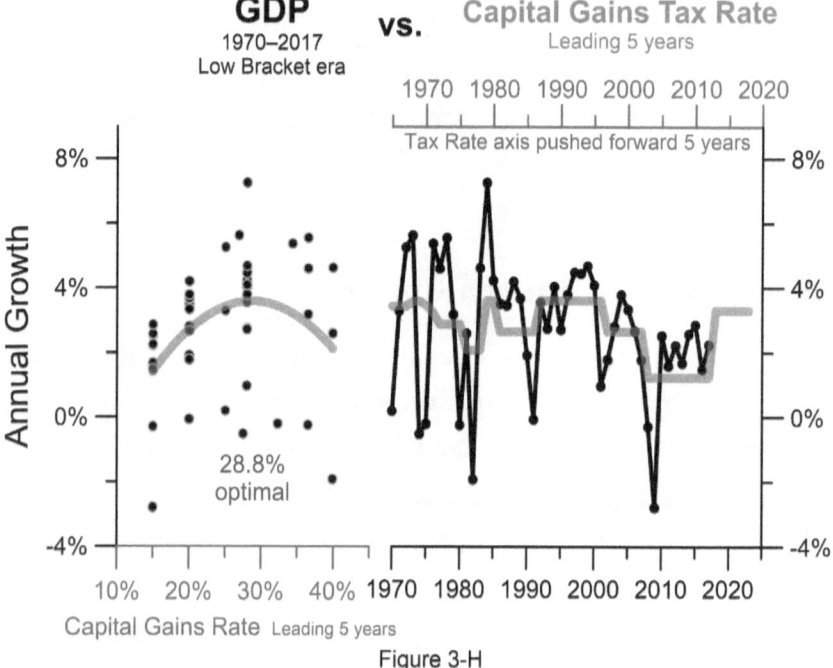

Figure 3-H

The long lead time of capital gain's influence on growth hides the impact from almost everyone. A couple years ago, a friend and I were talking about economics and politics at the Palo Duro Club pool. He, like almost everyone else, believed lower tax rates are good for growth. I asked him why he thought President Clinton, after raising taxes his first year, had a faster growth rate during his eight years than President Reagan.

He said something like, "I don't know how he did it, but the strong growth under Clinton was because of Reagan." I actually agreed with him, but didn't say so because I wasn't sure how to put it in context without a chart like Figure 3-H. Reagan raising the capital gains tax rate back to the near-optimal 28 percent greatly aided growth under Clinton. On the other hand, Clinton going along with cutting it back to 20 percent in 1997 harmed growth under President George W. Bush.

The back-to-back recessions of 1980 and 1981–'82 corresponded to the tax rate being too high at 39.9 percent. The Great Recession and financial crisis correspond to it being too low at 15 percent.

The official capital gains rate was raised back to 20 percent in 2013, but there is also a capital gains Medicare surtax of 3.8 percent as part of the Affordable Care Act, a.k.a. Obamacare. So the rate is actually 23.8 percent. This corresponds with a 3.3 percent growth rate on the gray best-fit line. President Obama raising the capital gains rate should make growth look good under President Trump beginning in 2018.

Trump initially proposed a 20 percent capital-gains rate, which entailed keeping the 20 percent official rate and ditching the 3.8 percent Medicare surtax. However, the Trump tax cut has left the 23.8 percent rate with an implied growth rate of 3.3 percent in place.

The best curvilinear fit in the High Bracket era suggests a 53.8 percent tax rate maximizes growth. The best statistical fit is definitely with the five-year lead time. The Great Depression corresponded with the 12.5 percent capital gains rate. The best growth corresponded with a 39 percent tax rate, which appears to have helped growth in 1941 and 1942. Brackets make a huge difference. The 39 percent rate that was harmful with a low bracket corresponded with the best U.S. growth ever at a high bracket.

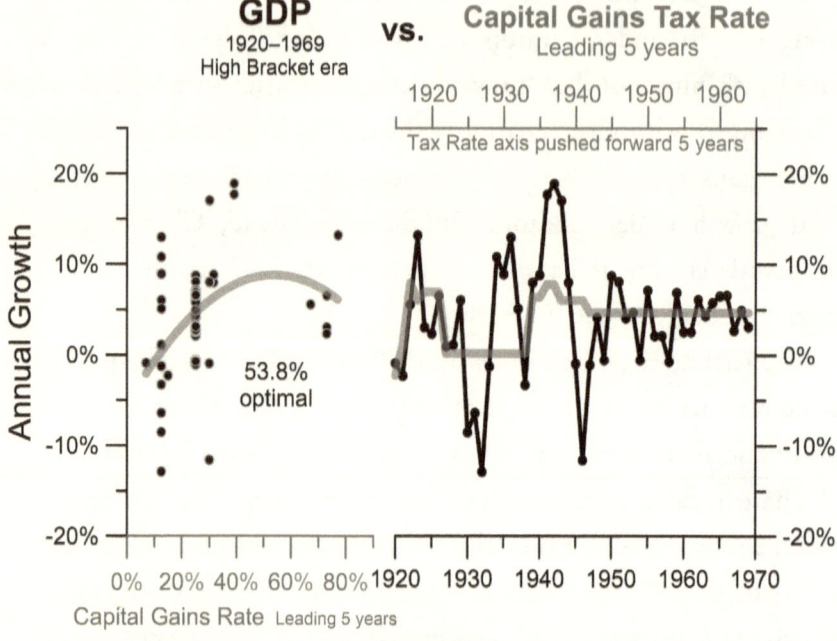

Figure 3-1

How Many Tax Brackets?

The number of brackets also makes a difference. For years I speculated that each tax bracket was a point of incentive along the income spectrum to avoid taxes by plowing money into a business, and that the number brackets would correspond positively with growth. The first few Internet searches did not turn up a source that listed how many brackets there were for each year; it was not a big enough priority that I wanted to track down each year individually.

About three years ago, however, another search turned up a page at the Tax Foundation which had them all. Sometimes laziness pays off—or, as I prefer to think about it, an aspect of genius is getting the best result with the smallest expenditure of resources or effort possible.

The number of brackets has ranged from two to fifty-six. Figure 3-J shows the expected positive correlation. I checked all the lead times from zero to twenty-five years. They were all positive, but there was no consistent pattern that clearly built to one lead time as the best. I ended up using the same three-year lead time as for the level of the top bracket.

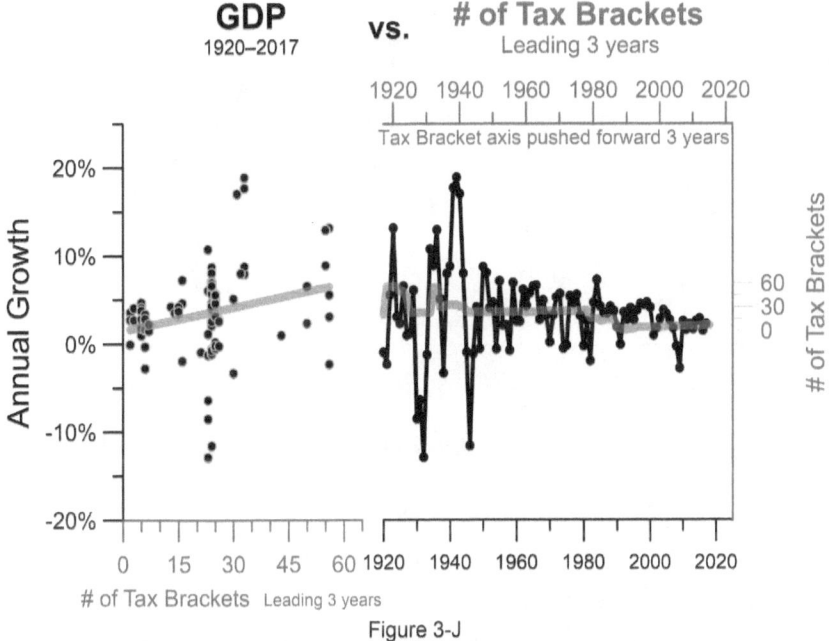

Figure 3-J

The seventeen years influenced by thirty or more brackets averaged growing 7.7 percent. Even if you exclude WWII data, the average is still high at about 5.5 percent. The three years influenced by two tax brackets averaged growing 1.8 percent.

If we look at the data since 1950 in Figure 3-K, the pattern is a little more orderly but the slope of the best-fit line is almost the same. The highest point on the chart represents the 8.7 percent growth in 1950 and the twenty-four brackets in 1947. The gray best-fit line suggests that with twelve brackets GDP would average growing 3 percent, and with twenty-seven brackets it would average 4 percent. More precisely, it estimates adding 15.5 tax brackets would increase GDP growth 1 percent.

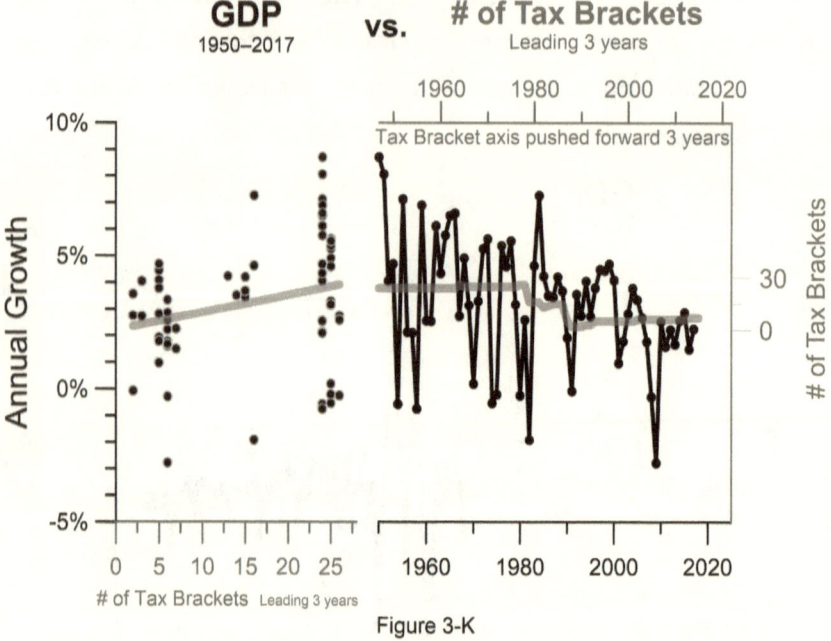

Figure 3-K

Reducing the number of brackets hardly simplifies taxes. Calculating the amount of taxable income requires enormous effort. Applying the tax rate or tax schedule to taxable income only takes a few seconds, whether there are two brackets or fifty. Computer software calculates it almost instantly.

Trump's tax cut left the number of brackets at seven which corresponds with 2.7 percent growth.

Corporate Income Tax

The corporate income tax rate appears to have little effect on growth. When I tested the rate against growth from 1920, the R-squared was only 0.01, or about 1 percent of the growth variation appeared to correspond to the variation in the corporate rate. The concurrent correlation was the best; the other lead times were weaker, and a curvilinear correlation was no stronger than the linear one shown in Figure 3-L.

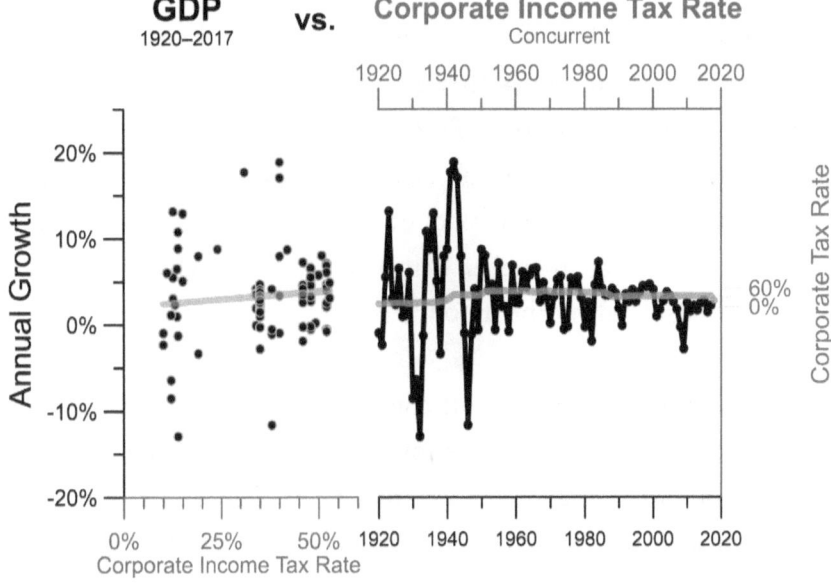

Figure 3-L

The correlation was positive, suggesting a higher tax rate meant higher growth. When I tested the data from 1950 forward, the positive correlation got stronger with an R-squared of 0.05, but this is still quite weak.

It then occurred to me that the higher growth when the corporate income tax was around 50 percent was due to other factors. When I controlled for the other tax policy variables we discussed above, the corporate tax rate had a negative correlation that optimized with a two-year lead time. When I say *negative* I mean that as the tax rate goes down the expected growth goes up. So while the expectation that cutting the corporate tax rate contributes to stronger growth has the direction right, it's still statistically insignificant in that the expected error from including the corporate income tax in a model was significantly larger than the expected signal.

Trump cutting the corporate rate to 20 percent should not affect growth much, but might help a small amount starting in 2020.

The proposed change in the corporate rate could greatly add to economic understanding. From an accounting standpoint, cutting the corporate rate will boost after-tax profits and benefit corporate shareholders (i.e., the wealthy). From an economic standpoint, this is not clear. In theory, much—or even *all*—of the burden of paying the corporate tax may be passed on to workers in lower wages and/or to consumers in higher prices, while the level of after-tax profits is determined by the amount of competition a corporation faces.

The corporate income tax cut could turn out to be a tax-cut for consumers *and* workers. It will be interesting to see the data and try and parse out what the effects are and when they occur. Perhaps after-tax profits will initially go up and then, after some lag, competition will bring them back down, while wages go up a bit faster and/or inflation rises a bit slower.

Cutting the corporate tax rate is worth trying.

The Model

When I put all this data together in a multi-linear regression model, the top tax rate, the capital gains rate, and the top bracket were all statistically significant. Apparently, enough of the influence of the number of tax brackets was already captured in the first three variables that it was not significant. The corporate rate does not appear to be a significant influence on growth by itself or in a model with the other variables.

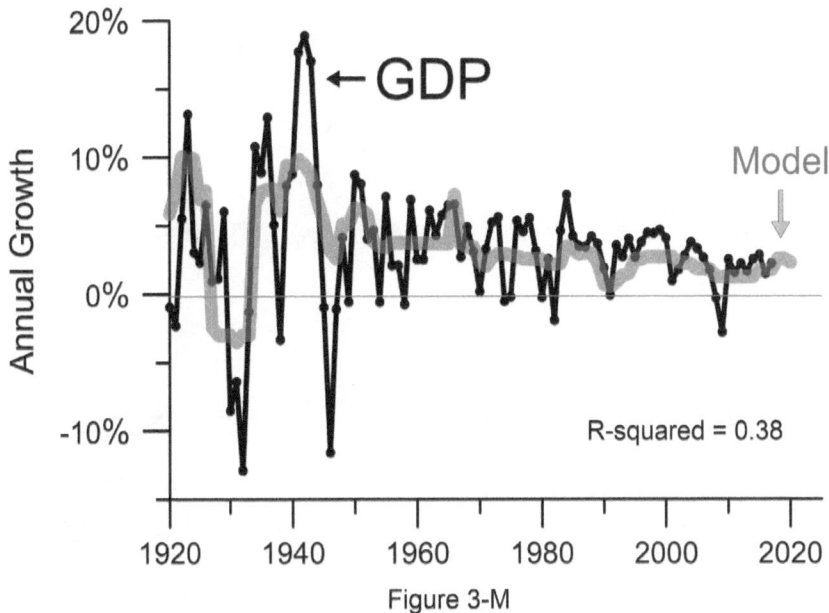

Figure 3-M

Much of the variation in the long-term growth rate appears to be driven by tax policy. Over seven-year periods, many of the other influences on growth balance out, including fluctuations of the business cycle. Figure 3-N shows the seven-year rate of growth and the estimate of the seven years by the model in Figure 3-M.

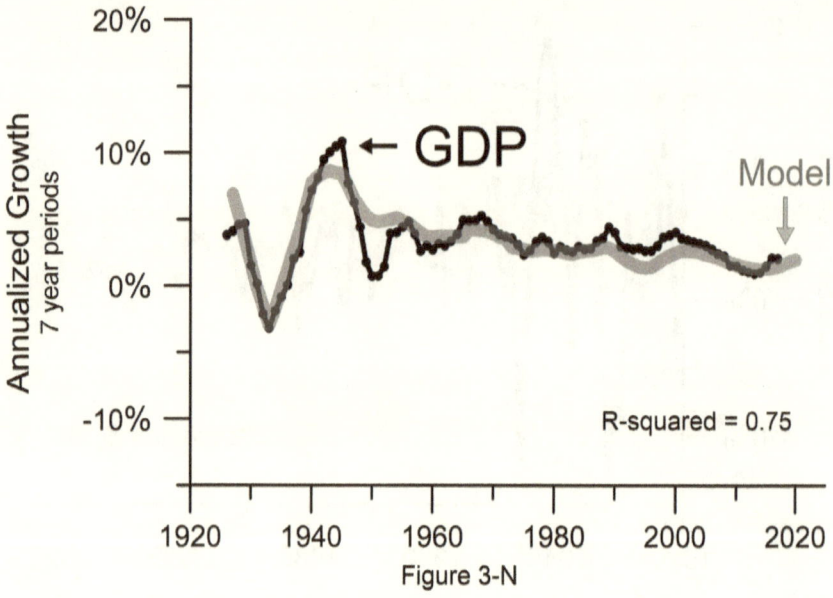

Figure 3-N

The influence tax policy gives our wealthy and talented to run—and *grow*—business appears to be a vital influence in driving the long-term prosperity of the nation.

In this chapter, we saw that the top tax rate and the capital gains rate can hurt growth if they are either too high or too low. We also saw that the income brackets these marginal tax rates apply to have a huge influence on whether the marginal rate is too high or too low. We saw that the top tax bracket measured in GDP per person (GDP/p) has been a eight hundred and fifty times higher than it is now. Trump raising it to $600,000 is positive, but to fulfill the potential growth it should go to several hundred million dollars.

The number of brackets appears to have a significant influence on growth—the more the better!—but when the other tax policy variables are controlled for, the number of brackets becomes statistically insignificant. The corporate tax rate appears to not affect growth much.

The important take-away: the combined influence of the top tax rate, the capital gains rate, and the top bracket appears to explain much of the variation in the long-term growth rate. The 25 percent top rate corresponded with the Great Depression. All of the periods that averaged growing faster than a 5 percent rate were influenced by a top tax rate at least as high as 50 percent and a capital gains rate of at least 28 percent.

You are on your way to understanding what we need to do as citizens and voters to restore prosperity. Chapters 4 through 8 will help grow the conviction for the needed action.

Chapter 4
Restore the Value of Work

In this chapter we will offer an explanation of why tax policy affects labor's share of the pie and how better tax policy might correct a mispricing of labor and improve growth. We'll make a logical argument for why the lead times of tax policy are so long. We'll consider ways a smaller share of the pie going to workers harms economic growth and point out weaknesses in the conventional theories of why workers should get a smaller share like they do. You will see the actual correlations with tax policy and a model that looks six years into the future.

We want capitalists and entrepreneurs to redistribute income through *work*, rather than our government treating the symptoms of low wages with social programs. We need a tax structure which encourages business owners to assign more value to work.

Distributing Income Away from Workers

In our current system, the CEOs who get the biggest performance-pay packages are often the ones who cut costs by laying off workers; on the other hand, I have heard business owners complain they can't find the workers they need. During an oil boom a few years ago, someone told me they would have liked to put more crews out on drilling rigs to drill for oil—but they couldn't find new employees who could pass a drug test.

Silently in my head I would complete the economic thought: "They couldn't find employees at the wage they were offering."

Looking at the short-term financial side of the economy, cutting worker costs makes a lot of sense: it gets good results in the short run and would be an even better strategy if your company were the only one doing it. If all businesses squeeze wages, however, the economy grows slower—both because there is less incentive for workers to produce goods and the lower wages paid mean lower sales for almost all businesses. Squeezing wages means less work, less motivation for work, and less money in the hands of workers to buy products.

The average real wage of non-supervisory workers hit its high in January 1973. While it has trended higher the last two decades, it's still about 4.7 percent lower than that 1973-high. Meanwhile, real GDP per person has more than doubled. So the share of the pie for non-supervisory workers dropped about 55 percent in the last forty-five years. Ask yourself: would you be more prone to anger if your place in society was downgraded by more than half?

Squeezing workers has economic and social consequences. In my Vanderbilt course, *Social Movements and Collective Behavior*, we learned that membership in the Ku Klux Klan surged during economic downturns and declined in times of prosperity. When times are tough and people believe they are getting less than their fair share, anger increases receptivity to ideologies based on blame, hate, and fear. Racial and religious violence likely spreads more easily in an economy that undervalues work.

Several years ago I read a *Fortune* Magazine article about what billionaires teach their children. One young man summed up his father's lesson on greed like this: "If you're doing a deal and your fair share is ten percent and you have the leverage to get eleven, take nine percent and ten more deals will come your way."

Business owners generally have more leverage in setting wages and salaries than employees or prospective employees. Therefore, the smaller share of the pie going to workers and a GDP growth rate less than half the norm from 2004 to 2017 may come from business owners and elites using leverage to get more in the short run, not realizing they are sacrificing their long run.

Our business schools have turned out many graduates with skills to cut costs—and labor is viewed as the *biggest* cost. If we want to create great wealth that lasts rather than a wealth that disappears in a bubble, we need our capitalists to think about the long-term real economy and prioritize the value of work. If you think of the economy as a carriage, labor and capital would be the two horses pulling it. If one of them is treated like an unwanted expense, it slows the carriage and makes it harder to stay on the road—regardless of how well the other horse is treated. Great wealth comes when capitalists partner with labor in a shared long-term vision of mutual prosperity.

Big Goals Require Work

To pull off long-term goals, a CEO needs a competent, motivated workforce with high morale which feels secure enough to take chances. If workers are afraid of the next layoff, they focus on protecting their backside—not advancing some vision from which they have no certainty they will benefit. Without workers engaged, wealth creation likely flops ... even if a few in management get huge bonuses for cutting costs and boosting short-term profits.

In Chapter 2 we mentioned Happy State Bank rose from the 812th largest bank in Texas to the eighteenth. Sam Silverstein writes about this in his book, *Non-Negotiable*. CEO J. Pat Hickman runs Happy State with twenty non-negotiable core values. Nine of Hickman's non-negotiables directly involve taking care of and empowering employees. Another seven relate to taking care of said employees.

Wages and Marginal Tax Rate Connected

In Chapter 1 we showed the decline in workers' share of the pie correlated with the top marginal tax rate. This is consistent with our theory that as the marginal rate comes down business owners pull a larger share of revenue out of their big pocket and put it in their small pockets, which leaves less money for workers.

In the 1950s and early '60s, when the top marginal rate was 91 percent, a very successful business owner could choose between nine cents of after-tax income and buying a dollar of labor in the business. As long as the dollar of labor added at least nine cents of value to the business, he was better off paying for more labor. If a wealthy woman could make the value of her business grow fifty cents with a dollar of labor, it was a huge bargain.

With a 91 percent marginal rate, business owners could not keep much gain from squeezing workers' pay. Growing the value of their big pocket in the long-term was the best path to wealth.

With a 29.6 percent marginal pass-through rate the potential to add to after-tax personal income from controlling labor costs rises dramatically. When money could come out of a business at the 15 percent tax rate for capital gains or qualified dividends, owners kept $85 for every $100 saved in labor costs.

In economic terms we would say the marginal after-tax cost of hiring labor goes down as the marginal tax rate on personal income goes up. Therefore, the demand for labor rises with the marginal tax rate. So if the top marginal tax rate goes up, demand for labor goes up and wages go up.

When higher marginal rates lower the after-tax marginal cost of paying workers, this may counterbalance the greater leverage employers have in negotiating wages. The higher economic growth rate that comes with higher marginal tax rates could be achieved simply by correctly pricing labor and unleashing markets to create prosperity.

In Chapter 12 we attempt to map out the higher marginal tax rates that will help the economy properly value work. In Chapter 1 we said we would deal with the six-year lead time being a plausible relationship between the top tax rate and wages shown back in Figure 1-B. Consider this: wages are sticky—they do not make big changes easily. Workers are loath to let them be cut and employers do not like to raise them. Workers will often stay in a job for years before the compulsion to look for higher pay pushes them to do so; labor contracts often last for years. It is reasonable, therefore, that pressure to cut or raise wages could build for years before significant changes take effect.

The Tax-cut for the Wealthy that Helps Wages

Remember in Chapter 2 where we said raising tax brackets reduced the average tax rate? Raising the top bracket also improves wages. In fact, the top bracket may exert the greatest influence on labor's share of all the tax-policy variables—or at least has the strongest correlation. We previously showed the correlation of the top tax rate with labor's share, but when we control for the top bracket, the top rate becomes statistically insignificant. This suggests the influence of the top rate is included in the bracket, which is reasonable as long as the top bracket and top rate are matched appropriately.

You may remember from Chapter 3 we are measuring the top bracket in multiples of GDP per person (GDP/p). Labor's share of the pie is very sensitive to the top bracket, up to about fifty-five times the GDP/p. On the scatter plot in Figure 4-A, you can see a steep slope of the gray best-fit line between 1 and 55 GDP/p. Above that level, labor's share is insensitive to the top bracket. This is shown by the best-fit line going flat between 55 and 300 GDP/p. On the right side of the chart, the flat gray line also shows where the GDP/p was above 55 and the share of the pie going to workers averaged around 50 percent.

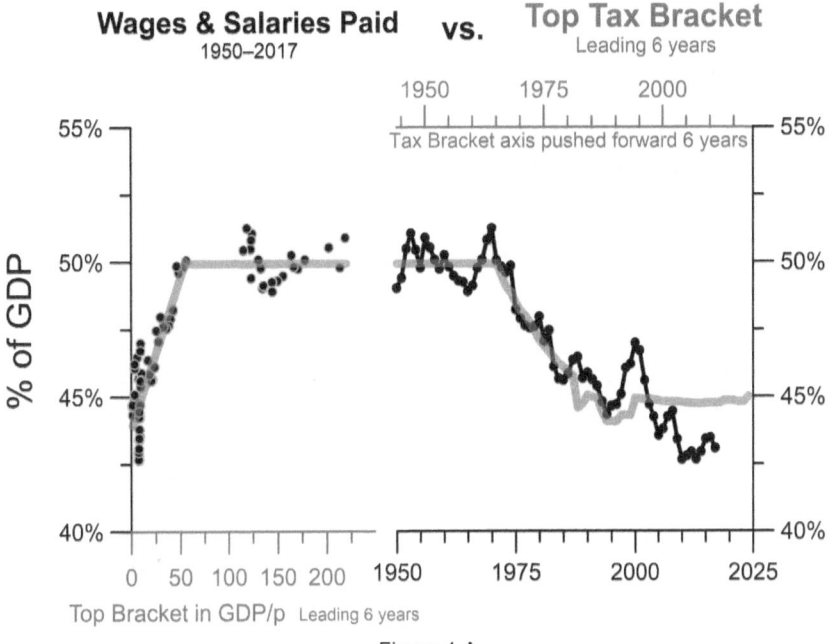

Figure 4-A

Based on 2017 GDP-per-person, a top bracket of 55 GDP/p for 2018 would be about $3.3 million dollars. If we want to maximize the incentive to work, we need a top bracket at least that high. Anyone serious about restoring the value of work should search for politicians who propose raising the top bracket to at least $3.3 million—and should *certainly* vote against anyone proposing to cut the top bracket.

As we showed in Chapter 3, a higher bracket would also benefit growth. A top bracket of several hundred million dollars would continue to improve growth without harming the incentive to work.

Capital Gains and Wages

The top bracket in recent years suggests the workers' share of the pie should be close to 45 percent. The influence of the capital-gains tax rate appears to be holding it down. The lead time for the capital-gains tax rate is a bit of a toss-up between six or seven years; Figure 4-B shows seven.

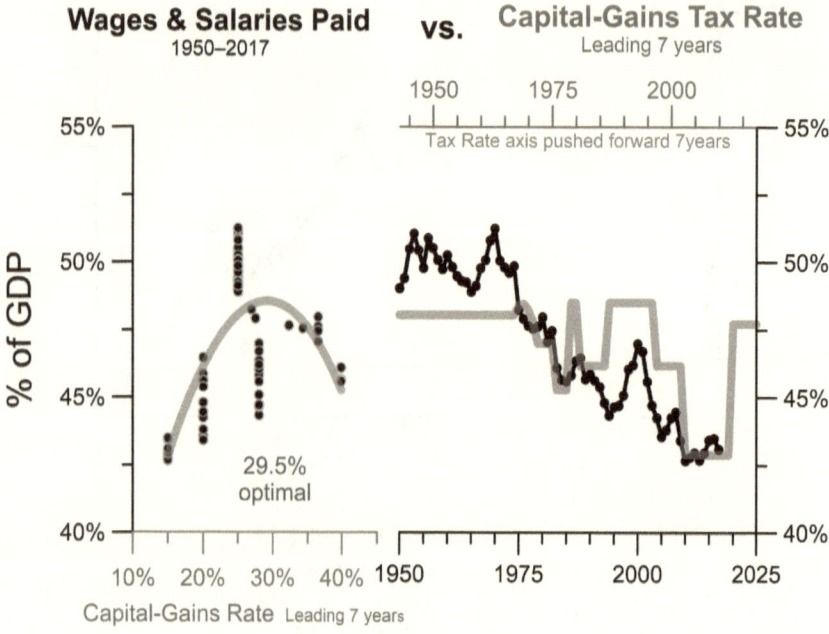

Figure 4-B

This shows a curvilinear relationship with the workers' share of the pie. The best-fit curve suggests workers are best off with a capital-gains tax rate of 29.5 percent, roughly the same tax rate that maximizes GDP growth in the Low Bracket era. The higher 39 percent capital-gains rate in the late 1970s corresponds with a weakening share for labor in the early- to mid-1980s. The great pain many workers have felt in the last few years corresponds with the smallest share of the pie to ever go to workers. A significant influence behind this small share is the 15 percent capital-gains tax rate.

While the chart above shows a capital-gains rate above 29.5 percent in fact harms workers, the highest top bracket in the period on the chart is about 219 GDP/p. When the top bracket was up in the 1,000s of GDP/p earlier in history, a higher capital-gains rate apparently did not harm the workers' share of GDP.

Wage Model

In Figure 4-C the model (gray line) shows the combined influence of the top bracket and the capital-gains tax rate. It suggests the workers' share will jump significantly in 2020 when the lagged effect of the capital-gains rate kicks in—although the boost could come in 2019, since the six-year lead time is also plausible. Sometime between now and then, a recession will most likely occur and the share will drop from its current level (just above 44 percent).

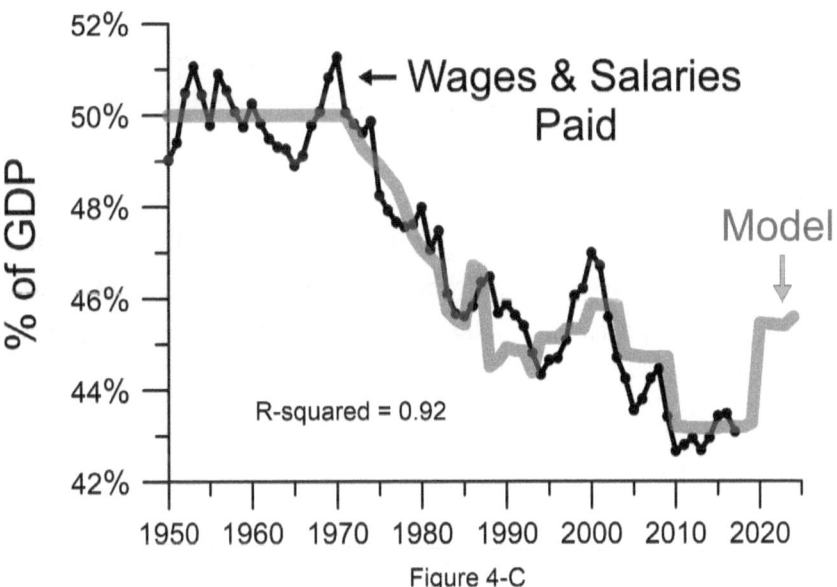

Figure 4-C

The Trump tax cut presents a bit of a cunundrem for this model. Raising the bracket should improve the share for workers starting in 2024, but lowering the marginal tax rate for business owners should harm workers starting in 2024. We will address this in Chapter 14 where we look into the future.

If workers had continued getting 50 percent of the GDP, the average worker would have taken home about $83,000 more the last ten years—and about $170,000 more since 1975. As we mentioned earlier, that is about $21.8 trillion.

The tax policies from Chapter 3 that were consistent with a 5 percent GDP growth rate should also move workers' share of the pie back up to 50 percent. The combination of the two would double workers' real income in about eleven years.

Don't Blame Technology and Trade

The people who got the $21.8 trillion instead of workers almost certainly believe they deserve it. If you had gotten part of it, you would probably think so too; conventional explanations support that belief. Business owners are probably unaware lower marginal tax rates increase their incentive to use their superior bargaining position to squeeze workers.

I may be the only one referring to this issue as the "workers' smaller share." Most people refer to it as "declining real wages" and blame it on trade, technology, robots, immigrants, Mexico, China, the Fed, Obama, Bush, or welfare programs. Has blaming Trump started yet?

The only one of these supposed "causes" that I could come close to correlating with the decline in the workers' share was trade. When I correlated the amount of trade as a share of GDP, it fit pretty well with the decline in the workers' share. When I put it in the model with the top bracket and the capital-gains rate, it was statistically significant, but less so than the two tax-policy variables. It did, however, bump the R-squared up to 0.93 from 0.92.

The problem with thinking trade affected workers is that the trade deficit, as you will see in Chapter 5, is also driven by tax policy. Business owners who put that $21.8 trillion in their small pockets instead of paying workers also padded their small pockets with several additional trillion dollars that didn't go for equipment, marketing, research, and such. All those trillions in the small pocket sucked in imports and drove up the trade deficit. When I controlled for the tax-policy variables that estimate the trade deficit, trade was no longer a statistically significant variable.

In this chapter we learned for workers to get more in their pockets, business owners first have to put more in their big pockets. As the marginal tax rate goes up, the after-tax cost of hiring workers goes down. So, theoretically, rising marginal tax rates should *increase* wages and cutting marginal tax rates should *lower* wages. The actual correlations with real data suggest this theory is true.

In other words, workers who earn less than the current top bracket of $600,000 and who vote for a politician who proposes to keep the current low top marginal rate or cut it further are voting against their best interest—*and* against the best interest of their co-workers, their families, and, as we showed in Chapter 3, against everyone's best interest in the long run.

Voting based on a slogan like "Cutting taxes will let you keep more of your hard-earned dollars," has historically meant encouraging business owner to keep more of what workers produce. Sure the tax cuts reduced what workers paid in tax, but they encouraged business owners to pocket $21.8 trillion that otherwise would likely have gone to workers.

We learned workers would get more in wages if the capital-gains tax rate were around 29 percent. We learned that trade and technology did not play a significant role in declining real wages over the last forty-two years. We learned workers should vote for politicians who will raise the top bracket to at least $3.3 million dollars.

Higher marginal tax rates may very well bring balance to the labor market and enable markets to unleash prosperity. The growth-optimizing marginal tax rate for $3.3 million is theoretically around 52 percent. You will see the basis for this theory in Chapter 12. But first, in Chapter 6 you will see how taking care of our workers helps maintain America's place in the world.

Now on to Chapter 5 to see yet another way low marginal tax rates weaken the American dream.

Chapter 5
Stop Selling America Out to Other Nations

In this chapter we will see why we can't remain a great nation forever if we consistently run trade deficits. We'll see the trade problem is not that we made bad trade deals or that our markets are too open, but rather that we have bad tax policy. We will look at the tax-policy variables with the greatest influence on trade, as well as the model made from those variables. We will see why this will give the first indication for President Trump's tax cut.

Excessive Consumption: The Path to Downfall

Warren Buffet compares a nation running a trade deficit to a wealthy farm family living a little beyond its means and selling a few acres of land each year to cover the difference. Gradually they exchange the life of a wealthy land owner for that of a tenant farmer.

When trade flows one way, ownership of assets flows the other. In the last forty years, citizens of other nations have bought $11 trillion of U.S. assets over and above what Americans have bought in foreign assets.

Foreigner nations now own about 60 percent of outstanding U.S. Treasury debt and about 15 percent of the U.S. stock market. The profits of Budweiser accrue to ImBev, owned by Belgium and Brazil; the Tata group from India bought the Landmark Pierre Hotel in New York City; Anbang Insurance Group, a Chinese company, owns the famous Waldorf Astoria Hotel; Chinese interests have also bought several U.S. businesses: Starwood Hotels, Smithfield Foods, Ingram Micro, General Electric Appliance Business, Terex Corp., Legendary Entertainment Group, Motorola

Mobility, AMC Entertainment Holdings—you can find more on the Internet.

In the 1980s, when we ran huge trade deficits with Japan, the Japanese were the big buyers of U.S. assets. For the trained economists who read this, let me be a little more precise: the net amount of assets sold to foreign nations is actually measured by the current account, and the lion's share of the current account is the balance of trade.

From 1977 to 2017, the trade deficit was $11.8 trillion. In those same forty-one years the current account deficit was 11.2 trillion. After trade, the next biggest item in the current account is net earnings: what U.S. citizens and entities earn on foreign assets they own improves the deficit, while earnings on U.S. assets owned abroad increase the deficit. So the billions of dollars China gets from interest on the U.S. Treasury Bonds they own and the profits from factories German auto makers own here weaken the current account.

Figure 5-A

Our current account has benefited from American companies acquiring many assets abroad at excellent prices after World War II. It remained positive longer than the trade balance, but it too eventually went negative.

What is true for individuals is also true for countries: If your outgo is more than your income, your upkeep will be your downfall. In 1977, the U.S. produced about 29 percent of the world's GDP. We are now down to about 24 percent, but our share of the world's consumption has not fallen as fast. The tax policy encouraging elites to load up income in their small pockets has hurt production in the big pocket, while encouraging more consumption with money piled into the small pocket.

While the top tax rate ranged from 70 to 91 percent Americans consumed about 60 percent of the GDP. Reagan's tax-cuts coincided with a trend toward more consumption and less savings and investment. The share of consumption reached 69.6 percent of GDP in 2017. Growing productive-capacity less and consumption more sucks far more imports into the country than we send out in exports. When the top marginal rate was higher, elites put more money into building businesses.

Consumer culture today glorifies overconsumption with TV shows like *Lifestyles of the Rich and Famous*. High consumption by the rich encouraged by bad tax policy may be setting a destructive example where the middle class and poor run up credit-card debt trying to follow in those rich footsteps.

Consuming more than we produce, skimping on building the future, and selling out assets to foreign nations paves the path to third-world status. Don't get me wrong—producing 24 percent of the world's GDP with only 4.3 percent of the world's population is a monumental feat. But we only gained this ability from standing on the shoulders of giants who plowed more into growing the future.

We have a long way to fall to get to third-world status, but we are on the path.

My great-great-grandfather J. A. Whittenburg, who built a huge fortune, had some advice that sounds foreign in today's consumer culture: If you are worried about what you should do, ask yourself, "Will it make a difference a hundred years from now? If not, don't worry too much about it—but if it will, move Heaven and Earth to make it happen." What we teach our children by example may have the biggest impact a hundred years from now. He taught his children and grandchildren, "We have enough money to buy everything we need, but not a nickel to waste."

A hundred-year time horizon means thinking beyond just what is good for you.

Will you build for the future or continue the example of going into debt to consume more? Tax policy influences consumption decisions and whether we run trade deficits.

Tax Policy Explains Trade Deficit

The top marginal tax rate and the capital-gains tax rate appear to explain most of the variations in the balance of trade, which has been racking up deficits continually since 1976. The top bracket and the number of brackets also correlate with the trade deficit in the expected manner—or at least the manner *I* expect—but when the top rate and capital-gains rate are controlled for, they are not statistically significant.

Trade appears to be the first thing tax rates influence. The lead times are just one year. Apparently, more income—or the expectation of pulling more income out of businesses—quickly leads to consumption. All consumers can relate to how easy it is to spend money. The top rate has a linear correlation and the capital-gains rate a curvilinear relationship. We'll look first at the top rate, then the capital-gains rate, and finally a model of their combined influence.

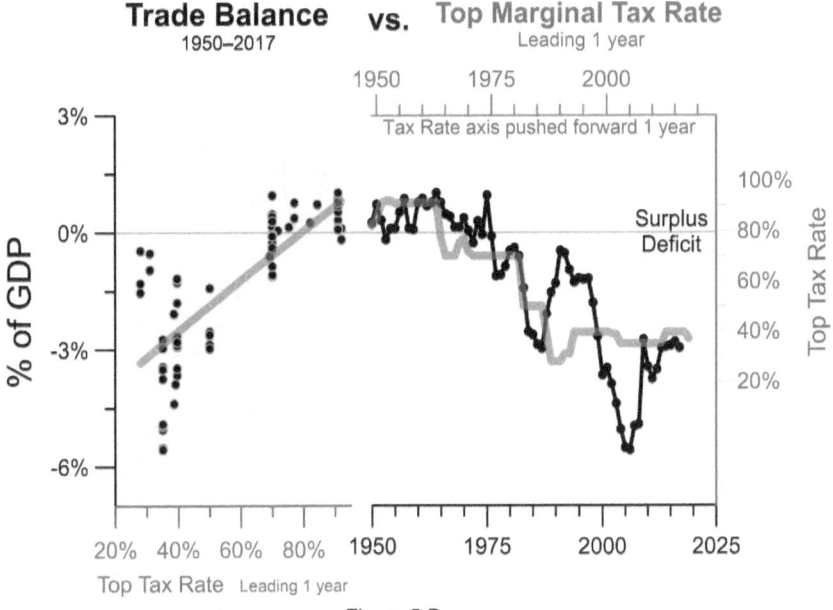

Figure 5-B

In Figure 5-B we look at the trade deficit as a percentage of the GDP instead of in billions of dollars. The gray best-fit line (in the scatter plot on the left of the chart) slopes upward, showing the higher the marginal rate the better the trade-balance is a year later.

Since this is a linear relationship, we can show how the actual tax rate corresponds to the trade deficit in the time-series line chart (on the right). You should notice that there have been no trade surpluses since the top rate was cut below 70 percent.

The capital-gains tax rate has a curvilinear best-fit line in Figure 5-C and suggests a tax rate of about 31 percent maximizes the trade balance. Sometimes, with a curvilinear fit, it is not easy to tell which points on the scatter plot match up to the points on the time-series plot.

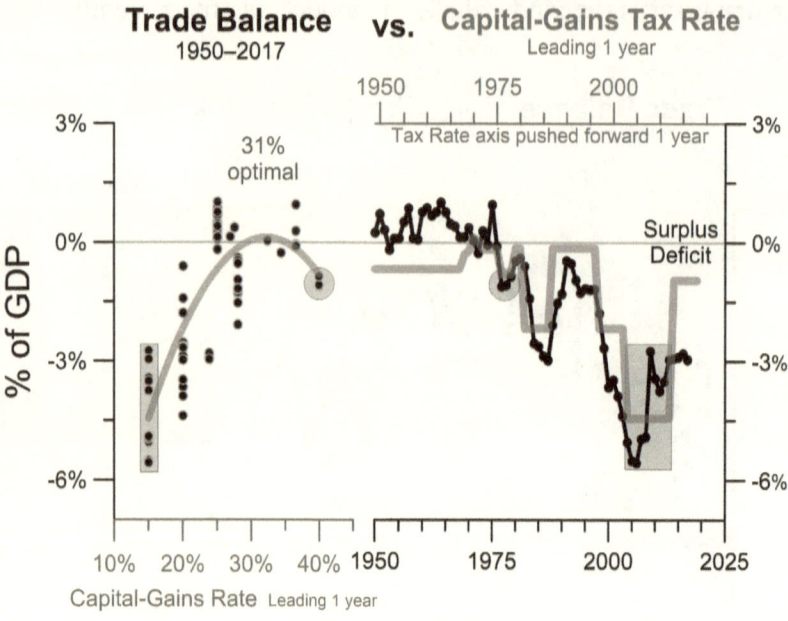

Figure 5-C

To help with this difficulty, I have circled the three dots on the left and right sides which correspond with the trade deficit influenced by a 39 percent capital-gains rate. I put rectangles around the ten years the 15 percent capital-gains rate influenced the deficit. The worst deficits came with the 15 percent capital-gains rate. The years with the best balance were influenced by a 25 percent rate and a 36 percent rate.

The best-fit line implies the years influenced by the 28 percent capital-gains rate should have had a better trade balance, but the unconstructively low top rate that also influenced trade in those years helped make the deficit worse. When we combine the influence of the top rate and capital-gains rate in the model, it appears to explain about 84 percent of the variation in the trade deficit as a share of the GDP.

While this is a reasonable conclusion from the data, it does not prove anything. There could be some other variable that, when accounted for, would make the top marginal rate and/or capital-gains rate statistically insignificant. I have looked for such a variable and have not found it, but that doesn't mean it's not out there. (Of course, this is true for all the models I have made—which is why I continue searching for data with influences and am eager to plot new data points as soon as they are available.)

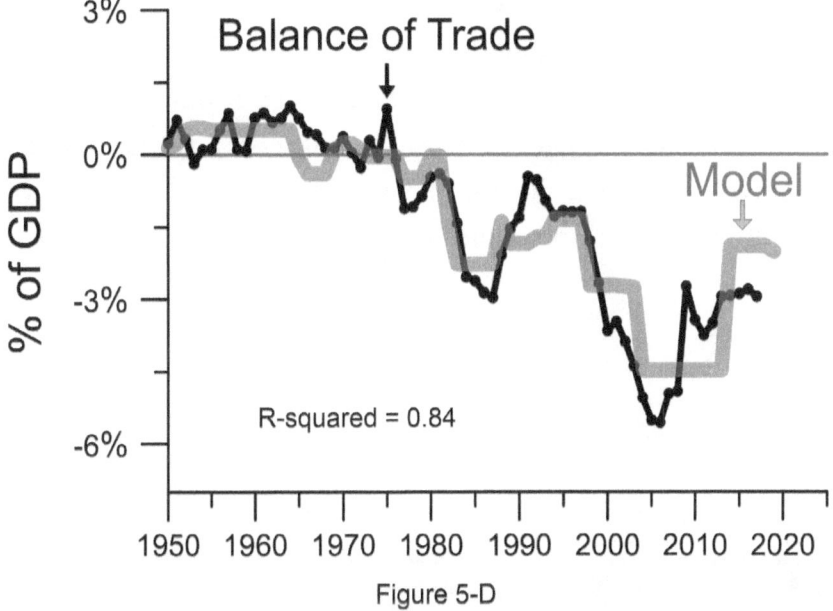

Figure 5-D

The next few years should provide an interesting litmus test of the conclusions above, especially since President Trump claims the trade deficit is due to weak negotiating by previous administrations and claims we can improve the trade deficit with tarrifs.

The balance of trade worsened in 2017 contrary to the forecast of the model. I hope, dear reader, you will watch with me as new data comes in. It should improve in 2018. If it does, count on Trump claiming credit.

All the Presidents I have watched claim credit for anything good that happens in the economy during their term. Whether Trump's expected claim is true will be better determined in 2019 and the following years when his 2018 tax cut should start influencing the trade deficit.

In this chapter we looked at the dangers of running a persistent trade deficit and how it contributes to our declining economic status in the world; more on that in the next chapter. We are not in danger of becoming a poor country anytime soon . . .

. . . but how long do we want to stay on that path?

We looked at the relationship of the trade deficit with top rate and capital-gains rate. They have impressive correlations and suggest we can eliminate the trade deficit with a higher top tax rate and a capital-gains rate. Since the lead times are shorter, the trade deficit data will give us the first chance to see any effects of Trump's tax cut.

Chapter 6
Our Place in the World

In this chapter we will see our nation's economic-status rises and falls in relation to how we treat our workers. Responsible consumption also matters. In other words, what we covered in the last two chapters relate directly to the U.S. share of the world's economic pie. We'll see that the capital-gains rate has a big effect on whether our business leaders view the economy from the short-term financial perspective or the long-term *real* perspective.

Figure 6-A shows U.S. GDP as a percentage of the World's GDP (as calculated by the World Bank). In 1960 we produced almost 40 percent of the world's output. Since then there has been a downtrend, with sharp fluctuations along the way.

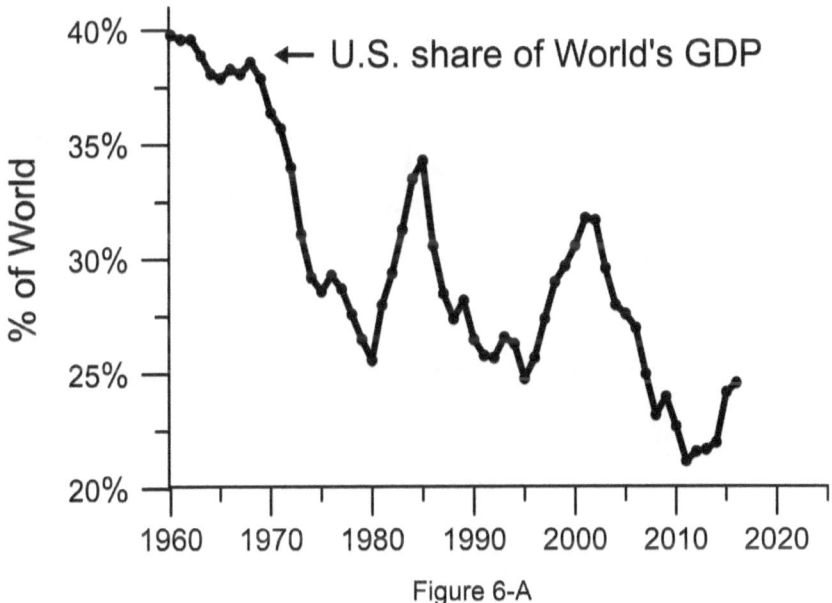

Figure 6-A

The next to last data point, 2015, was the strongest year of U.S. GDP growth since 2005. While 2016, the last point, had weaker GDP growth the rising dollar still improved our place in the world.

Necessity of Treating Workers Well

I could have built a model for the U.S. share of world GDP from the tax-policy variables like I have done in previous chapters, but instead I would like to drive the point home that our nation's status in the world fluctuates with how we treat our workers. Figure 6-B shows the relationship between the model of U.S. workers' share of the economy from Chapter 4 with the U.S. share of the world's economy.

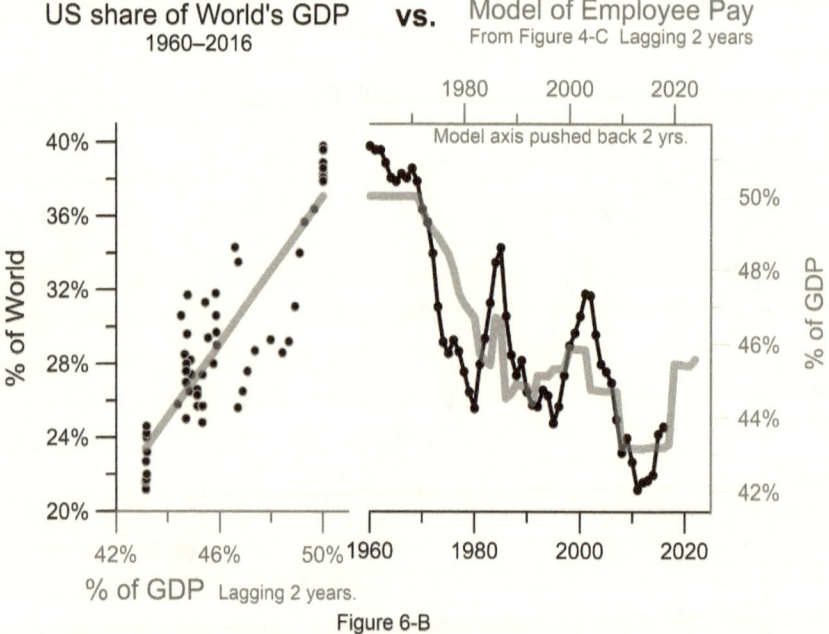

Figure 6-B

The tax policy that hurts our workers share of U.S. downgrades our standing in the world two years sooner. This is shown with the model of worker pay having a two-year lag time in Figure 6-B.

From the long-term real perspective, workers are the heart and soul of a nation's economy.

A strong nation requires a strong, well-compensated, motivated workforce. If we want to keep the nation strong we have to take care of workers.

Just as a company must keep its workers happy to keep customers happy, a nation must take care of its workers to maintain its place in the world. To enhance the long-term viability of a business when a downturn comes, you protect your employees. Back when workers' share of the U.S. pie was around 50 percent and the U.S. share of the world pie was close to 40 percent, the bond between company and worker often included loyalty. Today you are more likely to hear: "There is no loyalty." When the downturn comes, companies now try to protect profits by cutting employees.

From the short-term financial perspective, workers are an expense; therefore, management boosts profits by cutting that expense. Some companies use the "golden number," which is the ratio of profit-to-headcount. As that ratio (or some similar measure) increases, so do executive bonuses.

Corporate Systems was one of the crown jewels in the Amarillo economy. It processed medical billing for clients all over the country. It was the third-largest private-sector employer in Amarillo. Guyon Saunders built the company using a twenty-year outlook and taking great care of his employees.

Guyon and I met at Rotary. His father, Guy Saunders, and my grandfather, Allen Early Sr., were two of the founding members of the Rotary Club of Amarillo in 1917. Guyon became an investment-advisory client in December of 1996.

Our biggest investment position at the time was long-term treasury bonds. I was forecasting the T-Bill yield would fall to 2 percent and the T-Bond yield to 4 percent. This was pretty radical at the time, to predict rates no one had seen since the early 1950s. Interest rates fell and we made money in the account, but not enough to keep up with the stock market. A year later, Guyon put the money with another of his advisors (who was also a skiing buddy).

After Guyon retired from Corporate Systems, Johnny Mize became CEO and oversaw readying the company to sell. Marsh & McLennan bought it and merged it with their Stars division, which had a similar, but inferior, product. That division became CS Stars.

Management shortened its focus to six to eighteen months and pursued a higher golden number. Layoffs in Amarillo soon followed. Responsibility for some business functions were mostly outsourced to India. Quality and profits suffered and the Amarillo part of the operation folded.

The demise of Corporate Systems was symptomatic of the 15 percent capital-gains rate and 35 percent top rate that enabled a short-term financial focus and encouraged pulling personal income out of businesses rather than building them. This bad tax policy also encouraged over-consumption and trade deficits.

Both of these effects link to America's place in the world.

Over-Consuming Darkens Our Future

Figure 6-C shows the correlation of the U.S. share of the world's economy with the trade model from the last chapter. While that model only led the balance of trade for one year, it leads our share of the world economy by six.

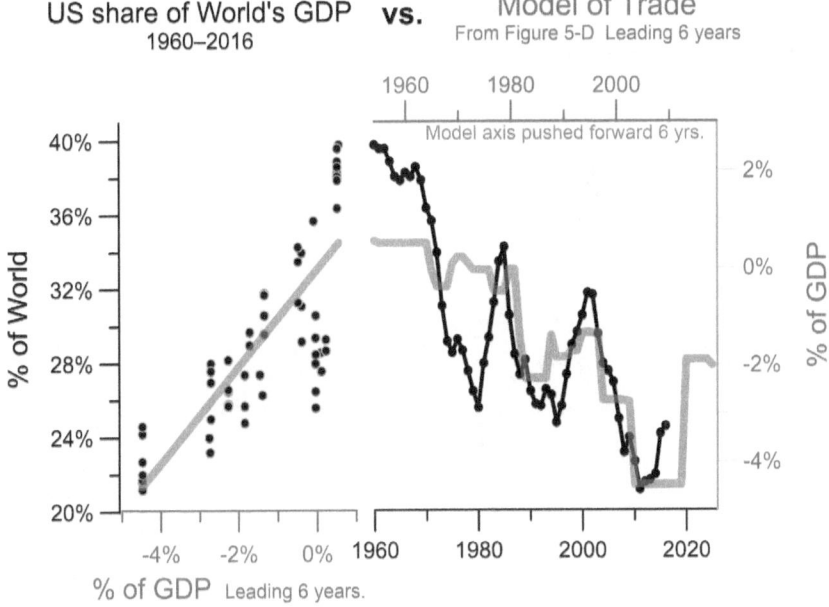

Figure 6-C

Over-consumption harms growth and our place in the world. Decades later, I still remember Dr. Getz's example in Econ 101. He talked about a primitive agricultural economy where next year's crop depended on the quality and quantity of the grain not consumed this year. The more you didn't consume meant more seed corn and potentially a much bigger crop next year. If you happened to consume the whole crop, you downgraded the economy from agricultural to hunter-gatherer.

This tax policy, which enabled consumption to jump from about 60 percent of GDP up to 68 percent and sucked in enough imports that we had to sell trillions of dollars of U.S. assets to foreign nations, downgraded our economic status in the world.

Figure 6-D shows the two models above combined into one model of the U.S. share of the world. Our share hit a low in 2011—probably its worst level since the Great Depression. The 15 percent capital-gains tax rate was a large factor in that low. As we discussed in Chapter 3, the 12.5 percent capital-gains rate played a major role in the Great Depression.

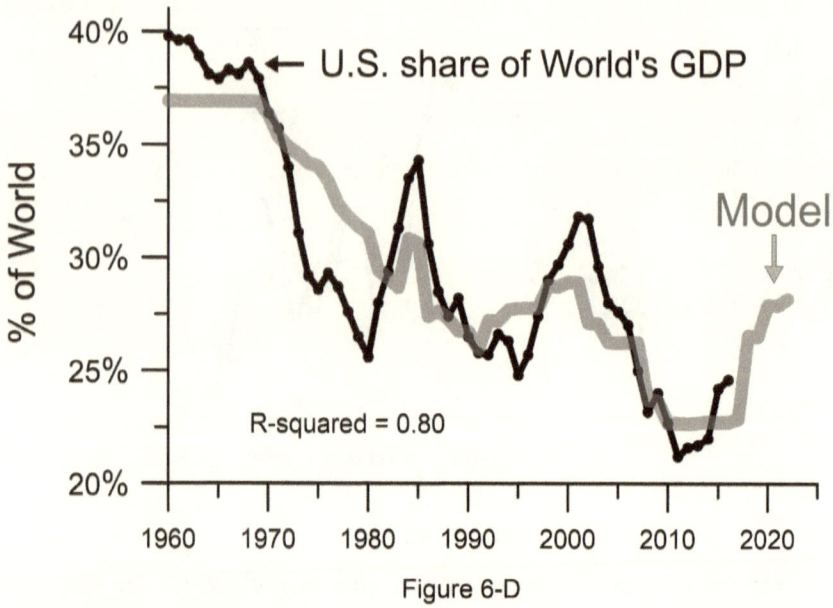

Figure 6-D

While I was not able to track down this data, I have heard it claimed the Depression took U.S. gross national product (that's GNP, not GDP) briefly below that of the British Empire (which at that time would have included India). I have also heard our industrial production dropping 53.6 percent to bottom out in July 1932 temporarily took us below German industrial production. While I am not sure those claims are true, additional data such as stock market returns suggests the U.S. suffered much more from the Great Depression than Europe.

Our rising share of world GDP from 2012 through 2016 was greatly aided by a rise in the trade weighted value of the US dollar. While the 2017 estimate of world GDP has not yet been released by the World Bank our share probably dropped since the value of the dollar declined 7 percent in 2017. The capital gains rate plays a huge role in the model. You may remember the model maximizing capital gains tax rate for labor's share of the pie was 29.5 percent, while 31 percent rate was best for the balance of trade model. Our economic place in the world should benefit from further increases of the capital gains rate.

The lagged effect of the capital-gains rate going from 15 percent to 23.8 percent should boost the U.S. share of world GDP beginning in 2018. With the different leads for capital gains in trade and employment, our model also estimates our share will grow in 2020.

The other two influences on this model are the top bracket and top marginal rate. The model indicates another small boost in 2022 due to Trump raising the top tax bracket to $600,000. However, it is possible the lower pass-through tax rate will instead lead to a decline that year. Remember: we learned in Chapter 4 that we want the bracket to go up to at least $3.3 million—or 55 GDP/p. We want an appropriate marginal rate for that tax bracket.

President Trump will claim credit for anything that goes well on his watch—as any politician would. The irony is that most of the expected improvement from 2018 through 2021 will likely be from Obama raising the capital gains tax rate. As with the other data, I will be watching to see how accurate the forecasts are.

In this chapter we learned that if we truly want to "make America great again," we need to make *working* great again. Our economic strength in the world rises and falls with how well we treat workers and how well we balance present consumption with improving production in the future. In the next chapter, we'll see how tax policy which is actually pro-growth will defuse the deficit timebomb.

Chapter 7
Defusing the Budget Deficit Timebomb

We will see that the Federal budget deficit and national debt are at least as much a growth problem as they are a spending problem. If we can restore growth instead of continuing to feed a ticking timebomb, the debt declining as a share of GDP could become a measure of improvement.

At a family dinner in 2005, I was visiting with a cousin of mine, Thomas Ratliff. He and his brother Franklin own DDD Exploration Inc. They develop oil and gas prospects and sell them to other oil companies, and occasionally individuals. They have been a part of discovering several new oil fields and producing multiple oil wells.

Thomas mentioned that Federal government revenue was at a new all-time high, which showed the Bush tax-cuts paid for themselves. He knew I hadn't thought the tax-cuts were a good idea. The claim surprised me. While I was downloading the quarterly government revenue into my data base, I was only examining it as a share of GDP. I didn't think it could be at a new high, but, knowing better than to argue with a smart man when you don't know the data yourself, I kept pretty quite.

He, of course, was right about the new high.

To feel like I understand the data, I want to look at the level, the highs and lows, the one-year growth rate, and the growth rate over a complete business cycle. I like to know where inflection points in growth are located. I want to understand how the rate compares to growth in other indicators. Sometimes I look at a thirty-six-year rate of growth, which is nine Presidential cycles and roughly the span between the peak of one baby-boom and the next. It's a rough estimate; the span between peaks varies a lot.

Revenue Growth

Later that week I analyzed the data. Federal revenue had moved strongly above the high set in the first quarter of 2001. I then wondered if it would still be higher after adjusting for inflation. At that point it wasn't, but it was a lot closer than I'd expected.

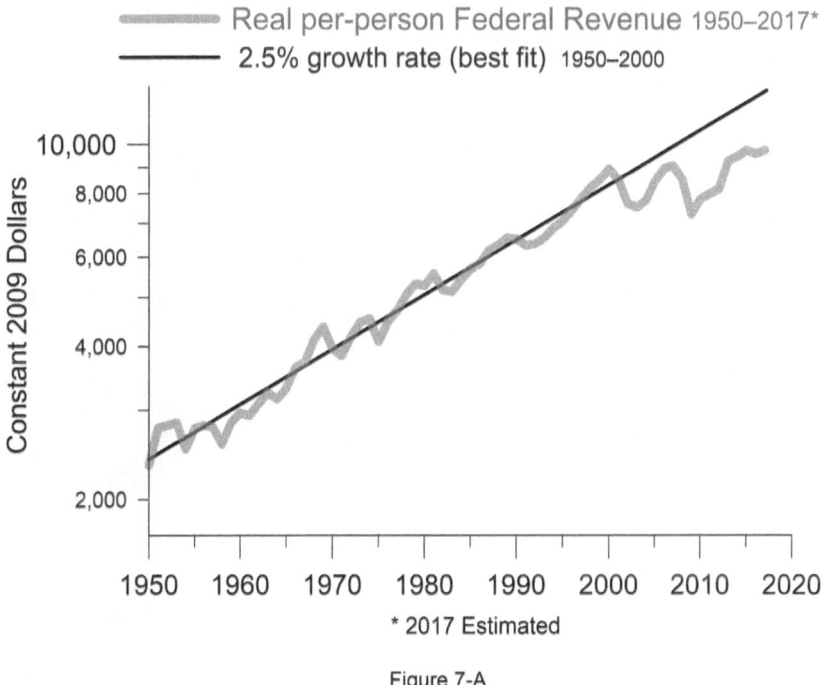

Figure 7-A

I silently asked myself what would make the best comparison. The idea came: adjust for inflation and population. In 2005, revenue measured this way was still well below the old high but was rising fast. From about 1950 to 2000, real Federal revenue per person trended higher, at about 2.5 percent a year. In 2005 it was not clear whether the surge in revenue would be strong enough to set a new high or regain the path of growth of the previous half century. I was doubtful the old growth rate would be reached.

Reflecting back, it was the 2005 discussion with my cousin and then my noticing the way-below-trend growth of real revenue per person that helped inspire me to examine tax policy's effect on GDP growth in 2006.

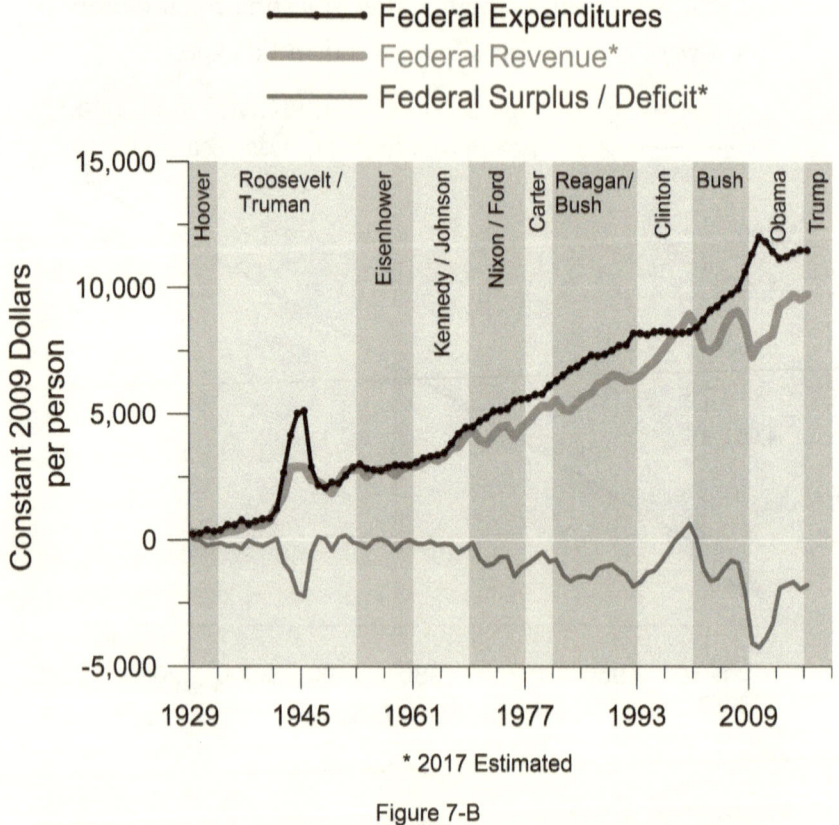

Figure 7-B

As it turned out, real revenue per person briefly reached a new high in 2007—but just barely. It's hard to see in Figure 7-A or 7-B. It did not reach the growth path of the previous fifty years. After 2007, it didn't rise above the 2001 level again until 2013 when tax rates went up. Since the 2003 tax-cut that took the top rate to 35 percent and capital-gains rate to 15 percent did not pass the Senate with a sufficient majority, they were set to phase out in 2013.

President Obama let most—but not all—of the Bush tax-cuts expire. After expiration, revenue surged in 2013 and has continued to grow (perhaps at a third the pace of the previous half century). We'll have a better gauge when we get a complete business cycle and can measure the growth rate from one business-cycle peak to the next, or one trough to the next. It's also useful to look at this data as a percent of GDP as Figure 7-C shows.

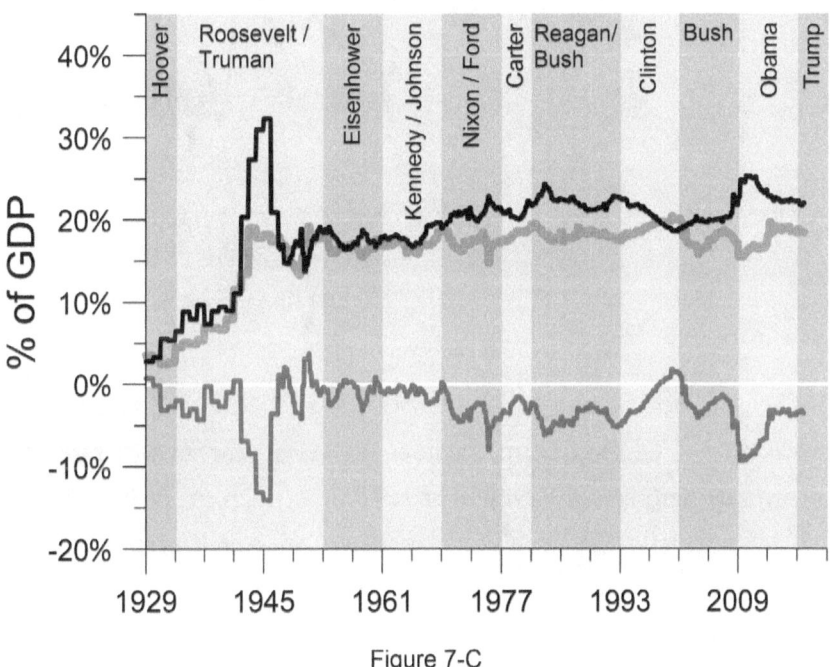

Figure 7-C

If the revenue had continued growing at 2.5 percent from 2000 and spending increased exactly as it did, we would have had Federal budget surpluses and President Bush (43) would have reduced the

Put Money in Your Pocket | 89

national debt. From the business-cycle revenue peak in 2000 to the one in 2007, real per-person revenue grew a total of 1.5 percent. If it had grown at a rate of 2.5 percent, it would have been 18 percent higher. Currently, Federal revenue is running about 18 percent behind spending. If revenue had grown at the historical pace, we would not have that gap.

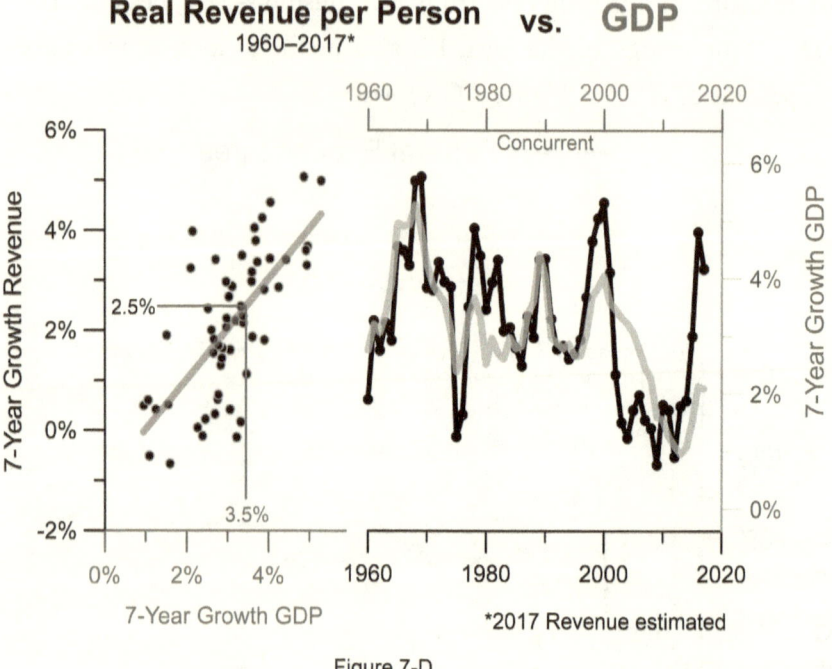

Figure 7-D

The gray best-fit line in Figure 7-D shows that, as the seven-year growth rate of GDP goes up, so does the seven-year growth rate of real revenue per person. Revenue growth hit 4.2 percent on the chart in 2016; normally this would be consistent with a 5 percent GDP growth rate. The revenue surge is not a sign of clear sailing, but rather a product of growing from a very low base in the great recession and being in the late stage of a business cycle.

When the next recession hits, this will not be as pretty a trend.

The best-fit line suggests if we could return GDP growth to 3.5 percent, real revenue per person would grow at the historical rate. I also tried this chart using one-year growth rates instead of seven-year rates, but it gave unrealistically rosy revenue-growth estimates. I think this is because one-year periods don't adequately model how recessions harm the growth in revenue. Using a seven-year growth rate means a year of weak revenue growth will show up in seven data points. This appears to make the estimate more aligned with the historical reality.

If we put in the tax policies that historically grow GDP at 3.5 percent or better, we should be able to grow revenue at the historical rate. If we could also hold the spending increases down to the level of population growth and inflation—as Clinton and Eisenhower roughly did—we would be able to balance the budget in about seven years without any drastic spending cuts. Spending cuts would make it happen sooner, but holding the increase to inflation and population growth would still be a political feat.

Debt Expansion

With real revenue per person trending flat or down from 2000 through 2012, the national debt tripled from 2000 to 2013. As a share of GDP, the debt went from 54.7 percent to 100.2 percent in 2013 and to 104.9 percent in 2016. This measure of debt ticked down in 2017 as the increase in the debt was smaller than the increase of GDP growth.

Figure 7-E also shows the debt as inflation-adjusted dollars per person. In 2017 it was about $55,000 per person, with inflation adjusted to a 2009 base. The surge in debt was influenced by a series of tax-cuts: the capital-gains rate went down in 1997, and there was a tax-cut in 2001 and 2003.

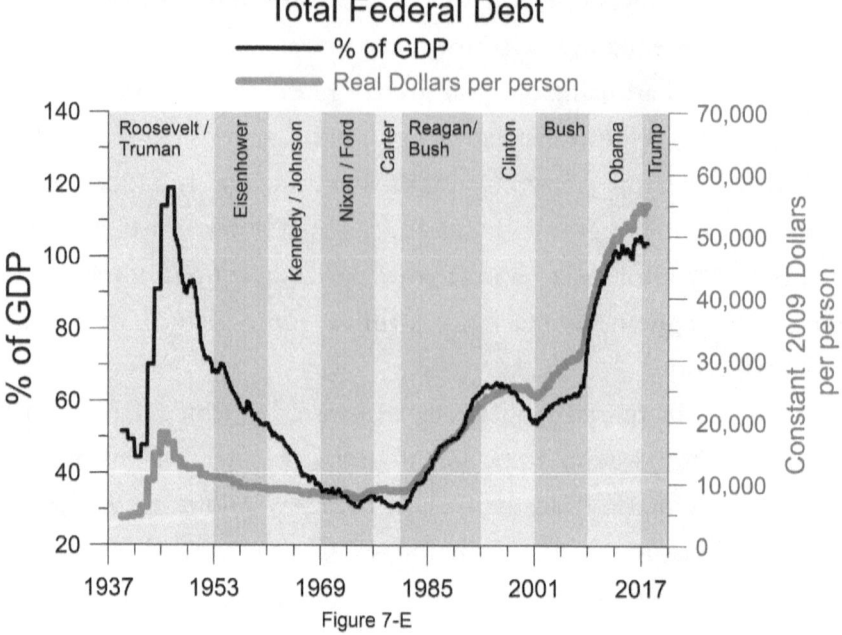

Figure 7-E

Since we survived the national debt being 120 percent of GDP coming out of World War II, we are probably not past some point of no return on a debt timebomb. However, the next recession will bring a critical turning point.

Trump Tax Cut Tees Up Crisis

The next recession will precipitate a Federal budget/debt crisis. A recession typically increases the budget deficit by 4.7 percent of GDP. For this stage in the business cycle we already have the largest budget imbalance since W.W.II. Debt as a share of GDP is pushing its highest level since 1947. Interest rates are rising and will increase the burden of the debt. When the next recession comes, the budget deficit will likely rise to at least 6.6 percent of GDP.

In the previous six business cycles the budget deficit averaged getting down to 1.38 percent of GDP during the expansion and rose to an average of 6.05 percent following the recession. The average increase was 4.7 percent. If you drop out the biggest and smallest increases the average increase for a recession was 4.5 percent.

At the end of 2017 the budget deficit was running at 3.5 percent of GDP. The lowest it got in the current expansion was 3.1 percent in the first quarter of 2015. That is 1.72 percent worse than the 1.38 average. In 2017 1.72 percent of GDP was $333 billion. So the budget deficit is about a third of a trillion worse in this cycle than normal. It is about $116 billion more out of balance than the worst of the previous six expansions.

So even before Trump's tax cut took affect we were in the worst fiscal shape in seventy years from both the standpoint of debt and a business-cycle-adjusted budget deficit.

David Stockman, President Reagan's budget director estimates the tax cut will reduce Federal revenue from the current 18.5 percent of GDP to 16.6 percent. He thinks Federal spending will soar since the sequestration agreement that held spending in check the for several years has been discontinued. Stockman expects a 2018 budget deficit well over a trillion dollars.

Trump's Treasury Department estimates the 2018 deficit at $400 billion, quite rosy compared to other forecasts. Chuck Jones in a Forbes article estimates the 2018 deficit will be near a trillion. Consider this scenario: The tax cut reduces revenue to 17.5 percent of GDP. Increased spending and higher interest rate costs on the debt raise spending from the 22 percent of GDP in the fourth quarter of 2017 to 22.25 percent for 2018. GDP grows at 2.5% in 2018, modestly faster than 2017. The budget deficit goes to 4.75 percent of 2018 GDP which would be $944 billion deficit, about what Jones estimates. The next recession could easily push the deficit to $1.5 trillion.

How voters and policy makers respond to the budget deficit during the next recession could define us as a great nation or a formerly great one.

Solve It with Growth

The path away from crisis grows the economy faster than the debt. If we can do that, the ratio in Figure 7-E would start trending down. If with good tax policy we returned the underlying growth rate to 3.5 percent, the economy would probably grow around 4 percent or better during expansions, and only shrink about 1 percent during a recession.

We have been through tax policies which gave us less than a 1.5 percent growth rate. This weak growth played out as growth falling to minus-3 percent in the great recession and only growing at 2.1 percent during the following expansion.

Since the 1930s, the economy has had some built-in stabilizers, like unemployment compensation, that appear to make recessions less frequent, shallower, and shorter. However, the deeper the recession, the more the automatic stabilizers drive up Federal spending. Faster underlying growth means less spending on such programs and faster revenue growth, which both slow the growth of debt. Remember that trillion dollars that didn't go to workers in 2016? With really good tax policy that shifts a trillion dollars more into wages and salaries, the demand on the social safety net should shrink significantly.

My analysis suggests the GDP growth rate one year has its biggest impact on debt the next year. Strong economic growth means slower debt growth. This inverted relationship shows in Figure 7-F, with a downward-sloping best-fit line and an inverted gray growth scale for GDP. The chart implies we should aim for growth of at least 3.4 percent to grow the economy faster than the debt.

In 2015, the inflation-adjusted national debt only grew 0.8 percent—the slowest since 2001, 2017 was almost as good. This does not mean we are out of the woods. This far into an economic expansion, real debt should be *shrinking*, not growing. When the next recession hits, the growth in debt will spike upward. In 2000, the real national debt shrunk 1.8 percent; then it spiked after the 2001 recession and had a much larger spike following the great recession. The growth rate in debt spiked to peaks in 2003 and 2009—six years after cuts to the capital-gains rate in 1997 and 2003.

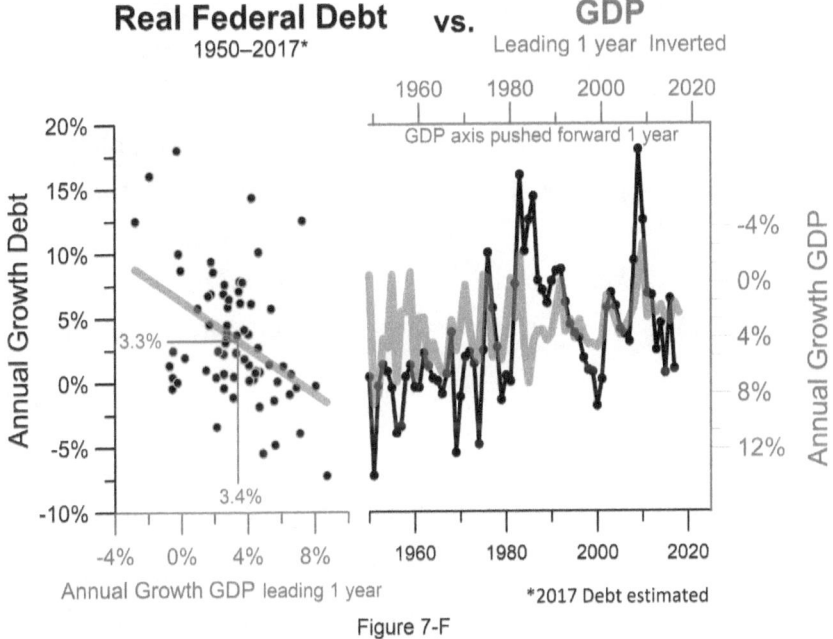

Figure 7-F

On the other hand, the big surge in debt in the early 1980s was more the problem of slow growth from the lagged effect of the capital-gains rate being too high—or at least too high for its bracket.

Ideally, we would balance the budget over the course of the business cycle; we should run surpluses in the late stages of an expansion to balance deficits during a recession. I thought we were on track to achieve this in 2000. I expected the 2001 and 2003 tax-cuts to throw us off track. Back then I didn't realize those cuts, along with the 1997 tax-cut, would slash the economic growth rate and take us this far off track.

As long as we start growing the economy faster than the national debt, as we consistently did from the end of WWII until mid-1981, the debt should not create any disasters. The top rate in this period averaged 80.6 percent. By contrast, the last thirty-six years where debt expanded faster than GDP the top rate averaged 38.3 percent.

The big takeaway from this chapter is this: if we return to tax policy that has corresponded with robust growth, we should be fine and not suffer much from the accumulated debt.

The Trump tax cut moves further away from that policy. It likely encourages pulling money out of the big pocket into the small pocket. We will need to watch economic growth, deficits and debt as we will likely march at a faster pace to explode a debt timebomb. Budget deficits in the next recession will be gut-check time for America.

The next chapter will look at another problem from bad tax policy—asset bubbles that threaten everyone's retirement security—and dive a bit deeper into the difference between the real economy and the financial one.

Chapter 8
Bubbles and Real Capital

In this chapter we'll see two ways bad tax policy contributes to inflating bubbles in the economy that later pop; we'll define "bubble"; we'll show the good tax policy that contributes to capital formation and hone the understanding of what real capital is. Understanding the difference between *real* capital and *financial* capital improves the chance our retirement security is backed by real value and decreases the chance it deflates just when we were counting on it.

An "asset bubble" refers to the price of an asset far exceeding its intrinsic value. Bubbles typically inflate via euphoria, where numerous market participants see a favorable trend in the price and, in their excitement, collectively bid the price far above the trend's reasonable conclusion. This happened with tech stocks in 2000.

A bubble can also form if market forces align to make the production of some commodity or real asset very favorable for an extended period. Eventually, production far exceeds demand and prices drop. This happened with the housing bubble, which peaked in 2006, and the price of oil, which hit $134 a barrel in mid 2008.

Bubbles: It's Tax Policy, *NOT* Interest Rates

The two bad tax policies that contribute to bubbles are 1) the top marginal tax rate is too low, and 2) a high marginal tax rate does not have a high-enough bracket.

A too low top marginal tax rate is practically the definition of a bubble. With a low top rate, lots of revenue gets pulled out of businesses as personal income. More money pulled out means less research, fewer and less-motivated workers, older equipment (perhaps with deferred maintenance), and slower implementation of new technology. The intrinsic values of businesses are weakened. In other words, the small pocket raids the big pocket. Hoards of cash in the small pocket can be used in the financial markets to bid up stock prices.

Perhaps the strongest example of this occurred between 1925 and 1932. When Coolidge dropped the top tax rate to 25 percent in 1925, the number of people taking million-dollar-plus incomes rocketed from seventy-five in 1924 to a whopping 207.

After the two year lag GDP only grew at a 1.1 percent pace in 1927 and 1928. Million dollar plus incomes surged to 290 in 1927 and 511 in '28. The stock market rose at a 31 percent pace those two years. Economic growth was actually strong in 1929 million-dollar-plus incomes ticked up to 513 and stock prices rose another 35 percent to the September high. Proof the small pocket had raided intrinsic value from the big pocket came with a forty-three month recession and an 85 percent collapse in stock prices.

Several asset bubbles in housing, gold, oil, bonds, and stocks have inflated the last twenty years and some have already deflated. The 1997 capital-gains tax rate cut along with marginal-rate cuts in 2001, 2002, and 2003 further enabled bubble inflation. I've never heard anyone else make a connection between low marginal tax rates and bubbles. Everyone seems to blame the Fed's low interest rates and quantitative easing for inflating bubbles. Yet other periods of low interest rates and quantitative easing did not lead to asset bubbles inflating.

Interest rates were about as low in the late 1930s and early 1940s as they got after the financial crisis. The three-month T-Bill yield averaged lower in the 1950s than it did as the tech bubble inflated in the 1990s. While the housing bubble was inflating into 2006, interest rates were comparable to the 1950s.

We know the low interest rates in the 1940s and '50s did not inflate huge asset bubbles because there were no asset price crashes that happened during or following that period. Higher marginal tax rates in the 1940s and 1950s encouraged elites to build value in their big pockets by growing businesses. They avoided pulling lots of money into their taxable small pockets, which might then be spent bidding asset prices into bubbles.

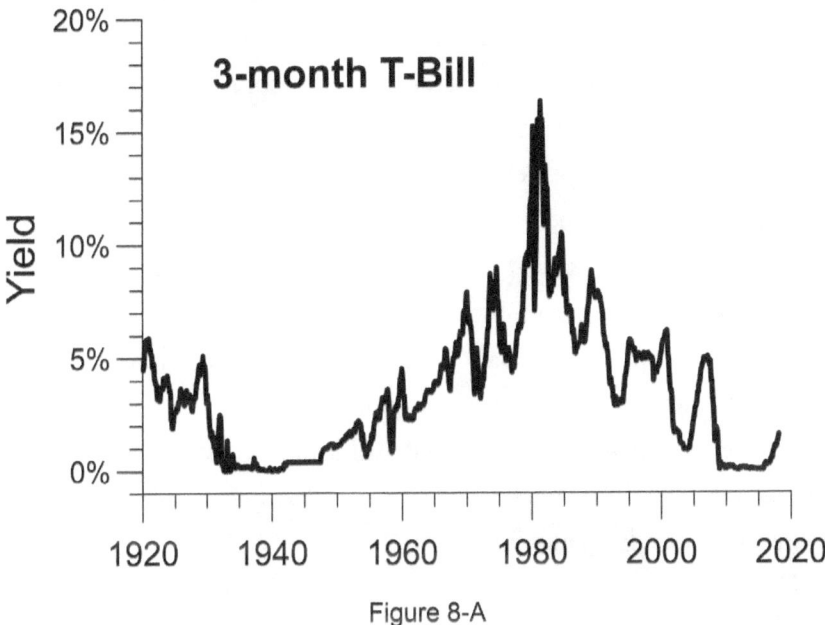

Figure 8-A

So if the marginal rate is too low, bubbles tend to inflate; but a higher marginal rate by itself is not the answer. A high bracket must accompany a high rate to encourage sound investment. If the bracket is too low, the high tax rate enables mal-investment, tax-shelter salesmen, or even fraud. (Low tax brackets probably turned some of the upper-middle class and much of the upper class into fodder for tax-shelter salesmen in the 1970s and 1980s.)

Mal-Investment Bubbles

When my parents came to visit my freshman year in 1978, we had dinner with one of my father's friends, a medical doctor who lived on a hill overlooking Nashville. We got into a discussion about investments and he said, "Doctors make some of the worst investors. They are so used to being the smartest people and so assume they know about investing too, and it opens them up to bad decisions." In retrospect I think this doctor had been sold lots of tax shelters that were designed to appeal to high-income individuals, but not to be good investments. The typical doctor or lawyer should not have to deal with a 70 percent tax rate.

The top rate of 70 percent was in place 1965-68 and 1971-80; its bracket of $200,000 started at 56 GDP/p. Economic growth and inflation whittled the top bracket down to about 21 GDP/p by 1978. As you will see in Chapter 12, a 70 percent tax rate may be too high regardless, but if we *are* going to have one its bracket should have been in excess of $100 million back in 1978. The 70 percent rate would probably have been good for growth—if its bracket had been high enough.

The combination of a high rate with too low a bracket encouraged lots of abusive tax shelters in the 1970s. Reagan cutting the top rate to 50 percent in 1982 helped growth significantly. However, the bracket for the 50 percent rate was still too low—it ranged from 6.1 to 10.5 GDP/p. Chapter 12 will suggest the growth-optimizing bracket for a 50 percent marginal rate is about three to five times higher at 31 GDP/p.

Richard Ware, president of Amarillo National Bank, remembers the 1980s as one of the frothiest investment periods of his career. Amarillo National is the largest family-owned bank in the country and has been in the Ware family for 125 years. It survived the Great Depression and everything else unscathed. There were lots of tax-shelter deals for apartments, office buildings, oil and gas prospects, and even cattle.

The early 1980s were boom times in Texas. In 1979, President Carter decontrolled the price of oil. The compromise to get it done was the "wind fall" profits tax. I remember my mother complaining in 1974 about the Arabs getting $12 a barrel for their oil, while because of Federal price controls she only got $3.50. Nixon tried wage- and price-controls to battle inflation for a couple years; they had dismal economic results and were lifted on everything except oil, natural gas, and gasoline. Remember gas lines and shortages?

When the price-controls came off, income from domestic oil and natural gas about tripled—even after paying a big chunk in wind-fall profits tax. The price of oil hit $40 in 1980 (or, adjusting for inflation, about $116 in 2017 dollars). Texas hardly felt the back-to-back recessions of 1980 and 1981-82. It was flush with cash, and tax-shelter salesmen were after it. President Reagan's 1981 tax-cut only brought the top rate down to 69.125 percent in 1981, but everyone knew it was going to 50 percent by 1982. So as long as you started drilling the well by December 31, 1981, you could deduct much of the cost at a high tax rate and then the income would be taxed at a lower rate. Active oil and gas drilling rigs in the U.S. hit their all-time high in December 1981. The rig count was more than twice as high as the peaks in oil booms of the last ten years.

Of course, oil *booms* are followed by oil *busts*.

The high price of oil had consequences. Consumption shrank—or at least grew at a slower pace. Production of oil shot higher from the boom in drilling. Oil started 1986 at about $26 a barrel, but dropped below $10 for a bit in the summer. A tax-shelter-style apartment complex was completed in Amarillo about then; it had almost no tenants, and the investors lost every dime they put into it. This was only one small piece in a much bigger problem.

The national savings-and-loan (S&L) crisis climaxed a couple years later. The Federal Savings and Loan Insurance Corporation (FSLIC) did not have enough reserves to cover all the failed S&Ls in the Dallas–Fort Worth area, much less the whole county. Ware remembers some of the failed S&Ls had assets worth only half the value shown on the books. To keep depositors whole while having time to avoid selling billions of dollars of assets at fire-sale prices, the Federal Government sold about $100 billion in Resolution Trust Corporation (RTC) bonds.

Pointing to one thing as the cause of any crisis involves, by definition, inaccuracy. Lax regulation, aided by corruption in Washington, some fraud, and low tax brackets, all contributed to low-quality or even junk investments cleverly packaged to avoid taxes. Whether you think of it as marginal tax rates being way too high or as tax brackets being way too low, many people became fodder for tax shelter salespeople in the 1970s and 1980s.

A small consolation was enough Texas bankers remembered the "froth" of the 1980s and so they participated less in the housing bubble that peaked in 2006. House prices did not fall much in Texas.

Housing Bubble: A Symptom, *NOT* a Cause

Some people believe the housing bubble caused the financial crisis and great recession. I tend to think the bubble was another effect of bad tax policy that led to weak growth.

Would the ratio of house prices to wages have been out of line in 2006 if the economy, jobs, and wages had grown as fast in the expansion from 2001 to 2007 as they did in the expansions from 1991 to 2001?

Using the idea I mentioned in Chapter 7 of measuring something over a whole business cycle, at the peak in 2007 there were 4.2 million more private-sector jobs than at the peak in early 2001. Between the trough after the 2001 recession and the trough after the great recession, 1.2 million private-sector jobs were lost. Averaging those two numbers out, I estimate that business cycle created about 1.5 million private-sector jobs. Using the same method, the previous cycle added almost 15 million—about ten times as many.

Workers' share of GDP rose to 46.9 percent in 2000. If workers had maintained that share through 2007, they would have had an additional $2.1 trillion dollars over seven years. An additional $2.1 trillion spread among existing workers and millions more new jobs would have gone a long way toward turning the housing bubble and crisis into a normal housing market. This is a reasonable case for the theory that the housing crisis was just another symptom of weak growth from bad tax policy.

However, given this weak growth, short-term financial thinking made the housing problem worse. Part of the reason policy doesn't do more to encourage long-term thinking is that people don't know what capital is.

What is *Real* Capital?

In the fall semester of my sophomore year at Vanderbilt, Dr. Malcolm Getz asked the class, "What is capital?" I thought I knew the answer: experience with investments started early.

When I was in second grade, my parents presented me with an opportunity. A few years before, my father and a partner went into the motel business. They built the Coronado Inn as a franchisee of the Master Hosts chain. Master Hosts International was offering to sell franchisees stock on favorable terms. My parents didn't have the money to buy any, but thought it was a good enough deal to ask if *we* wanted to. My sister and I were interested; my brother, not so much. I put up most of my savings—about $200—and my sister, who had more years of getting cash gifts from grandparents and perhaps was already earning an allowance, put up two or three times that much, and we bought a hundred shares.

Over the next several months the price went up. Occasionally, my mother would tell me the price. It was usually higher than before. Eventually I got excited and started asking for the price. It had more than doubled. Then once I asked the price and it was lower. I started asking the price almost every day. It felt to me like it was declining. I wanted to sell, but Mother encouraged me to hang on. After a few weeks of saying I wanted to sell, my sister and mother relented and we sold. I got about $400—double my investment. Not bad for a seven-year-old.

I'm not sure what happened to Master Hosts International—whether it was acquired, changed its name, or went under—but the next year the economy was heading into recession and my overextended parents lost the motel to the bank, along with all my father's assets which had been collateral.

Despite a few years of relative hardship, the experience inspired my interest in money and finance. I read my first book about the stock market in eighth grade and joined an Explorer Scout group on finance by the ninth grade.

Given all this experience, I was shocked when Dr. Getz's first example of real capital was "a dump truck!" He was driving home the point that real capital is capital-equipment used in producing goods and services. Real capital includes machine tools, industrial robots, computer servers, office buildings, the electric grid, and, of course, dump trucks. It's not stocks and bonds—it's *equipment*.

The misperception of capital plays into the wrong-headed convictions of tax policy's influence on capital formation. Sure, low marginal tax rates help the wealthy accumulate more financial capital—but at the cost of less real capital formation.

How to Avoid *Junk* Investment

The best measure of business investment in productive capacity is probably fixed private non-residential investment. I show this as a percent of GDP in Figure 8-B, along with a model I made similar to the other models.

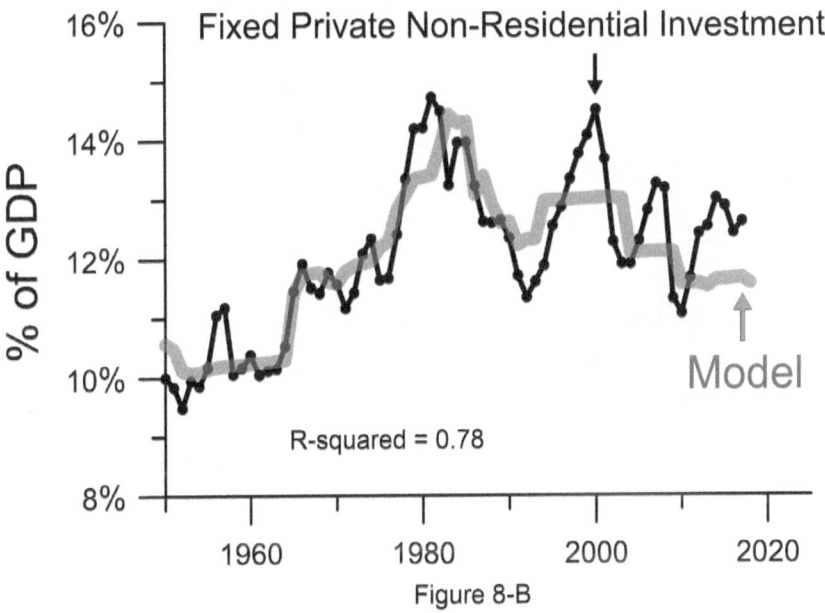

Figure 8-B

Unfortunately, this measure does not show the quality of investment. It doesn't distinguish between investments that drive future prosperity and those that mainly avoid taxes. Investment as a share of GDP peaked in 1981, the same year the rig count peaked. The growth coming out of that peak investment was significantly lower than growth in the early- to mid-1960s, when investment was much lower.

Since I'm not impressed with this measure, I won't show all the charts of indicators behind the model; but there are a few things worth noting. The top tax rate and capital-gains rate had the expected positive relationship where higher tax rates led to more investment, with lead times of one year and seven respectively.

The top tax bracket had a negative relationship. At first this surprised me and I kind of ignored it, since it didn't fit my expectation. I've learned the hard way that ignoring things that don't fit expectations can be dangerous. It now makes perfect sense that, as the top bracket deteriorated from 136 GDP/p in 1960 to 17 in 1981, that investment would go up—but that low brackets increased junk investment.

Lots of people suffered from bad investments in the '70 and '80s. In the late 1980s and early '90s I published a paid subscription newsletter, *ECONOMIC LEADS*. In about 1989 I called someone at Securities Research Company, which produced the large chart of the stock market I had on my office wall. I wanted to rent some names from their mailing list to test for marketing. He was mad someone from *Texas* was calling. It took several minutes for him to realize I wanted to be his customer and that I wasn't trying to sell him an oil and gas deal.

The big takeaway for me is that we want every marginal tax rate to have a high-enough bracket that it doesn't drive people to make junk investments—people who lack the sophistication to reliably make quality ones.

On the other hand, for the people who have a multi-million or -billion-dollar portfolio of businesses, we want high-enough marginal tax rates that it's in their best interest to make quality investments that will drive prosperity for the nation. We are talking about people like Warren Buffet or the sharks on CNBC's *Shark Tank*. We're better off when these people grow their wealth by making deductible or depreciable investments that build the economy. We want these people to have huge reasons to avoid taxes.

This, of course, means higher marginal tax rates. You have probably heard, "If we raise tax rates it will drive capital out of the country." When you hear this, remember that it is important to distinguish between *real* capital and *financial* capital. The statement might be true for financial capital, but may be the exact opposite with real capital.

Tax-cuts Killed Manufacturing Jobs

Manufacturing jobs depend on real capital. The series of tax-cuts from 1997–2003 was followed by real capital fleeing the country. The marginal tax rates went from a 39.6 percent top rate and 28 percent capital-gains rate to 35 percent and 15 percent respectively. The average of these two, at 25 percent, was the lowest since the Great Depression when it got down to 18.75 percent. In Chapter 5 we talked about how low tax rates led to foreign nations buying U.S. assets. In addition to Treasury bonds the Chinese also bought many U.S. businesses. A lot of the manufacturing businesses the Chinese bought were packed piece by piece and shipped to China.

Perhaps you recall from Figure 5-C the capital-gains tax rate leads the trade deficit one year. After the capital-gains tax rate was cut in 1997, the next year the trade deficit increased and the number of manufacturing jobs declined, 1998 was the first of twelve straight down years. We lost a third of our manufacturing jobs in those twelve years; the number went back to a level last seen in April 1941.

Manufacturing jobs are more capital-intensive than most other jobs. It's interesting to note the other big tax-cutter of our time, President Reagan, who cut the capital-gains tax rate his first year in office, also saw a loss of manufacturing jobs. He came into office in January 1981 with 18.639 million and left eight years later with 18.057 million. If you are like me, reading those numbers should shock you, since otherwise Reagan had strong job growth. It's easy to see for yourself if you simply Google "MANEMP." The first item in the search should be "All Employees: Manufacturing | FRED | St. Louis Fed." Clicking on this link will bring up an interactive chart of manufacturing jobs. It is easy to move the pointer to a month and see the number of jobs, as well as to download all the data for yourself.

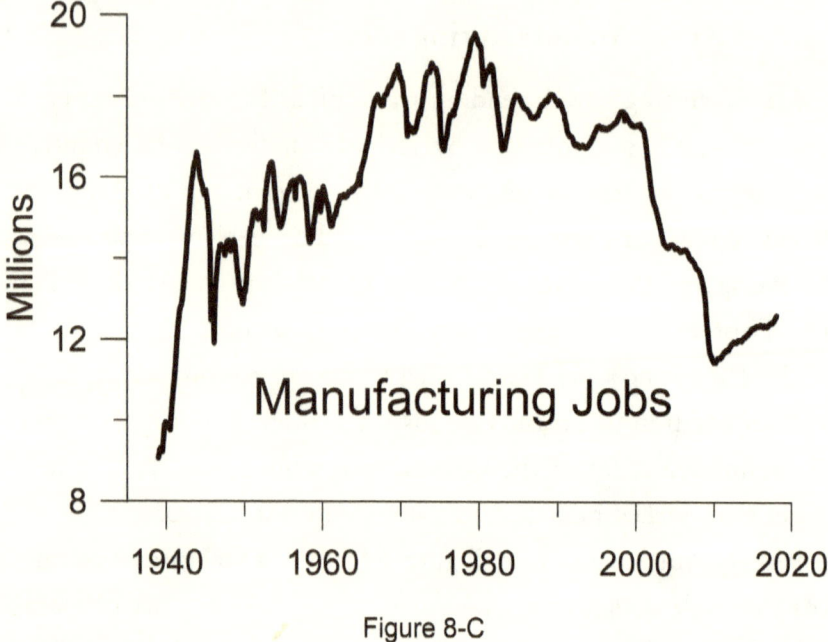

Figure 8-C

President Trump's tax cut should start harming growth in the economy and manufacturing jobs in about 2020. I hope you will join me in tracking this going forward.

Someone I met the summer after the financial crisis drove home the difference between real capital and financial capital. I was visiting my sister at the Gipsy Trail Club near Carmel New York; I had swam the half mile across the little lake to one of the small floating platforms and struck up a conversation with Jacky Beshar, who was also resting there. She and her husband Scot Jones own Groov-Pin Corp., which makes industrial fasteners used by BMW and Toyota. The company has been around since 1926 and has sold billions of grooved pins, including about 100,000 in every Boeing Dreamliner. We talked about the economy and the financial crisis we'd been through.

She told me about a Morgan hedge-fund manager she'd met the summer of 2008 who was pulling in several times the income she and her husband were making in manufacturing. She was a bit curious—if not disturbed—that it should be that way. During the crisis this manager, who no longer had the "Master of the Universe" attitude, told her, "You are so lucky. You have real assets."

If we want more real assets we must realize raising marginal tax rates will not harm real capital or cause it to flee the country. It may inspire a few people who want to live off income from financial assets to leave, but these are not the people who create our future prosperity.

If someone wants to retire abroad where tax rates are lower, we should wish them well. If we have a sound tax system that encourages real capital formation, our future will be secure. If the real capital stays and a bit of financial capital flees, we'll just make more and its value will be backed by actual productive capacity—rather than euphoria that dies as a bubble pops.

A Super Bubble?

A process similar to the 1920s, but at a much slower pace appears to have occurred the last twenty-eight years. The 1986 tax reform took the top tax rate to 28 percent in 1988, which would have started influencing growth in 1990. The top tax rate has not been above 40 percent since. GDP has grown at 2.4 percent from 1990 through 2017, almost a third below the normal pace. Meanwhile stock prices after dividends and inflation rose at about 12 percent above the normal pace.

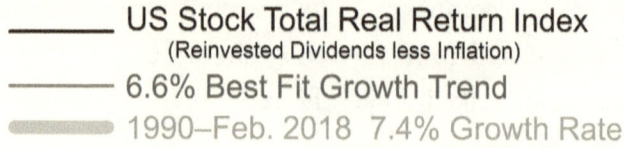
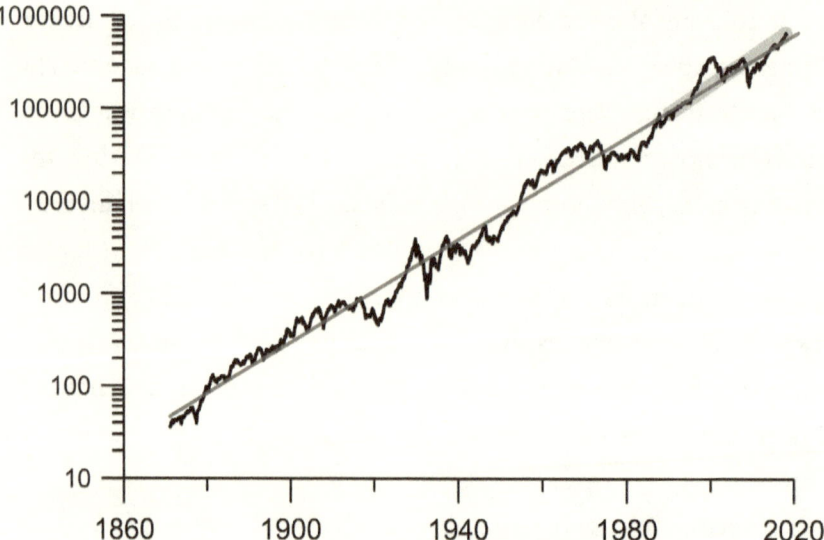

Based on S&P Statistical Service as reported earnings, Cowles and Associates, Common Stock Indexes and Bureau of Labor Statistics' consumer price index.
http://www.econ.yale.edu/~shiller/data.htm   http://us.spindices.com/indices/equity/sp-500

Figure 8-D

In 1990 the valuation measure I use for the stock market was at the level that was average prior to 1990. Valuation then went on a ten year surge. In 1996 when the valuation was roughly at or above the level of all previous stock market peaks Fed Chairman Alan Greenspan described it as irrationally exuberant. Since then valuation has averaged more than twice what it averaged prior to 1990. At the stock market bottom in March 2009 valuation almost made it down to what was normal prior to 1990.

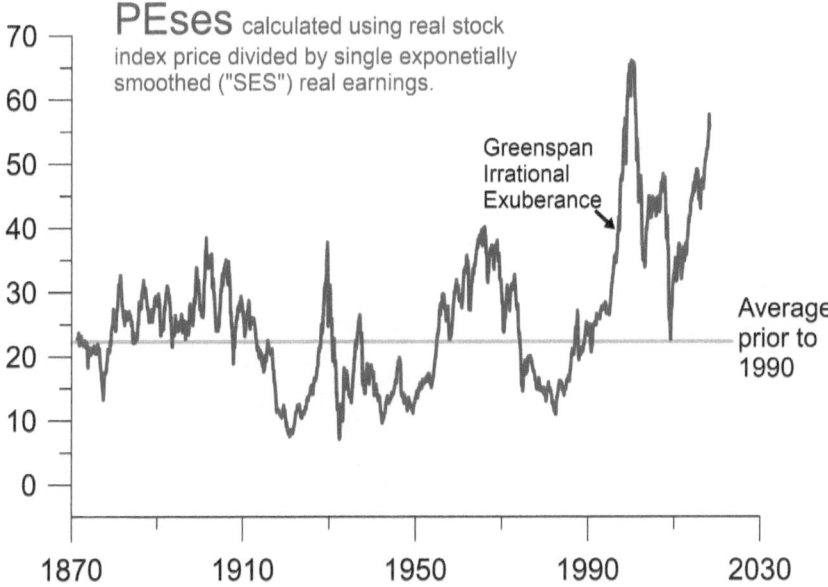

Figure 8-E

The PEses that I use is similar to the cyclically adjusted price multiple ("CAPM") that Dr. Robert Shiller of Yale uses. The difference is that instead of the ten year moving average of real earnings that Shiller uses I use single exponential smoothing ("SES") as recommended by Bob Bronson at Bronson Capital Markets Research.

One of the problems with a ten year moving average is that sometimes the tail wags the dog: a change in the average could just show what was happening ten years ago. Exponential smoothing has heavier weights on recent data. Historically, PEses has a stronger correlation with future stock market returns than CAPM.

Most of the analysts and advisors (including me) who expected stock market valuation to return to what use to be normal have looked silly being too bearish and given bad advice the last ten years.

In January 2018 PEses was 159 percent above what use to be normal, 426 percent above the 1982 low and 711 percent above the 1932 low. The sixty-four trillion dollar question is whether the last twenty years is a new normal that will endure or a super bubble that will revert to previous lows and if so, when?

I still believe there is a super bubble in stocks and that below average economic growth and above average stock market returns and valuations are all the result of low top marginal tax rates encouraging elites to pull more money out of businesses and using the money to bid asset prices higher.

However, I have found reasons higher valuation is partly justified. For example, stock market valuation tends to be highest with a 2.3 percent inflation rate. High inflation is hard on stock market valuation. Deflation is hard on stock prices. The rate of inflation since 1990 has averaged 2.4 percent very close to the goldilocks 2.3 percent.

GDP growth also appears to have a goldilocks rate of inflation. Chapter 10 shows a chart for it.

I expect the Trump tax cut will further inflate the bubble and pop it. If GDP growth continues at a below average pace and the stock market resumes its above average rate of advance following the correction in early 2018 I will interpret this as blowing the bubble bigger. There could be several violent multi-years moves in stock prices, both up and down between now and 2025. If it is a bubble I expect it will have fully deflated by 2025, but the bottom will likely not have a PEses valuation as low as in 1982 or 1932.

By the way don't take any of this as investment advice. Before making investments consult an advisor or do your own research.

Summary

In this chapter we learned low marginal tax rates contribute to asset prices inflating into bubbles. And if brackets are too low for a high marginal rate, it leads to junk investment and another kind of asset bubble.

All bubbles eventually pop.

Manufacturing jobs correspond with real capital, not financial capital, and cutting marginal tax rates can and did decimate manufacturing jobs. High marginal rates with high brackets lead to sound investment and growth. Encouraging the top 0.01 percent of society to grow businesses may be the key to prosperity and financial security. We don't need to worry about real capital fleeing the country if marginal tax rates go up.

While several bubbles have popped in the last twenty years, asset prices may still stretch above intrinsic worth. The Trump tax cut could further inflate asset bubbles and bring a climactic pop.

In the next chapter we'll see how the misperception about taxes persists.

Chapter 9
Paradigm Blindness

Here we will see why the economics profession, the financial media, and just about everyone else fails to see the reality of how tax policy affects the economy.

Where on Earth do I come up with the audacity to claim the economics profession suffers from paradigm blindness?

It all started at recess at Saint Andrews Episcopal Kindergarten. One of my best friends—John Barfield—and Mrs. Teel were inside working on some project. The boys divided into two teams to play war. All of a sudden two people from my side defected to the other side and we were down to three. Not long after, it was just me. I think I was given the chance to join the other side, but somehow it didn't seem right. Despite a hard run it didn't take long for nine boys to catch me. They dragged me over to the jungle gym. Four of them held me down, one on each limb. Some of the others took turns climbing the jungle gym, jumping down, landing a few inches to a couple feet away, and saying something like, "Oh, I missed him—let me try again."

I knew they weren't going to hurt me. These were good boys. Three of them were in my car pool. Still, the idea of everyone being against me crushed me emotionally. I cried over this: all the way back to class, during part of the class, that night, three nights later, three *years* later. I think I channeled this pain on the second day at Crockett Junior High. Looking for a seat in the cafeteria, I saw one next to a friend from elementary. It turned out to be the jock table—not really where I belonged. One of them distracted me while another took my carton of milk. From the facial expressions around the table, it felt like the whole table was in on the joke. Tears are not a good way to start junior high.

About twenty-five years later, standing in the sanctuary before church, I had an epiphany. The kindergarten experience was gentle preparation for a time when I would need to stand up for something where it would seem everyone else was on the other side. In one moment the experience that I thought might have scarred me for life became a source of strength for which I was grateful. I learned at least three lessons: 1) don't get too wound up in unpleasant circumstances, because they might be blessings in disguise; 2) what something means to you is defined by the context you see it through, and you are responsible for choosing that context; and 3) it is never too late to have a happy childhood.

So I am not afraid to play the role of the young boy who shouts, "The emperor has no clothes!" or "Low marginal tax rates hurt growth!"

Trapped in the Box

Higher education is a box. The box packs marvelous lessons, tools, and wisdom. Our society benefits greatly from this box, but reality does not stop at the edges of advanced degrees. In fact, the box can make some concepts harder to see.

Gisele Gowin Duehring began studying mechanical engineering at Iowa State University in the late 1970s. Her "Intro to Problem Solving" professor began the class with an apology: "I'm sorry. I'm sorry for what we're going to do to you. If I were to give you a major world problem to solve today, you would probably come up with a dozen different solutions. However, by the end of this class, you may only come up with three once we teach you about constraints and laws and limits. Unfortunately, we are probably going to educate the creativity out of you."

Albert Einstein says, "Imagination is more important than knowledge." When he developed his most important contribution to science, the theory of relativity, it was rejected by the established scientific community. His Nobel Prize was for a smaller achievement, the photoelectric effect.

In turn, when Einstein was an elder in the scientific community he tried to hold back Max Planck's advances in quantum mechanics. Planck later said, "A new scientific truth does not triumph by convincing its opponents and making them see the light, but rather because its opponents eventually die, and a new generation grows up that is familiar with it."

To paraphrase: "Science advances one funeral at a time." At least in this regard economics could be considered one of the sciences.

In my own experience, once you believe something it becomes way too easy to dismiss conflicting evidence. In 2010 I had a nineteen-year record of outperforming the stock market after fees for my investment-advisory clients. I was convinced the measure of stock market valuation mentioned in the last chapter that got down to what I thought was average in 2009 would soon plunge toward the 1982 low. I believed an extreme level of valuation would be followed by the opposite extreme within eighteen years. I didn't understand there was a context where valuation could go to twice the historical level and remain there for twenty plus years or perhaps indefinitely. Clinging to a belief lead to significant underperformance, cost me a number of clients and almost the entire business.

Sincere beliefs do not guarantee correctness.

Missing the Importance of Brackets

Here is what gives me confidence: economic PhDs are blinded by the box. They don't see the importance of brackets in tax policy.

In Chapter 3 you saw the correlations of the top bracket with growth. You saw the bracket made a difference in what top marginal tax rate was best for growth. You can probably imagine that if all your earnings above $40,000 were taxed at 66 percent then you wouldn't have much incentive to work to earn more than $40,000. With a bit more imagination you could picture owning three-dozen businesses with the potential to pull a $500-million income out. If the marginal rate hit 66 percent at $400 million, you might conclude you would be better off spending that extra $100 million on startup costs for several new businesses rather than pay another $66 million in tax.

So you can see that whether the bracket is $40,000 or $400 million makes a huge difference in the growth effect of a 66 percent marginal tax rate.

So far, the economic literature does not see this. The economic literature does not examine tax brackets. OK, let me be more precise: after logging many hours at the West Texas A&M University library (it's the closest institution to me with subscriptions to the databases of the economic literature) on multiple occasions over the course of eight years, I found only one economic paper on selecting tax brackets for marginal tax rates.

It was published in 1948. Gabriel Preinreich's paper, "Progressive Taxation and Proportionate Sacrifice," had to do with setting a bracket for each marginal tax rate at a level where each income group would have a comparable sacrifice to their standard of living. While I could have missed something, it appears no economist has asked the question, "Do tax brackets influence economic growth?"

Tax brackets apparently aren't in any of the economic models taught in higher-level economics. In the papers about influences on the long-term growth rate, there was no mention of the incentive the marginal tax rate gives business owners to put money in their big pocket. This concept that Chapter 3 suggests dominates the long-term growth rate is not rejected by the literature—it isn't even examined.

The several dozen papers I examined in the literature promoting the idea that lower marginal tax rates improve growth were all based on economic models. The formulas purporting to show a low top rate improved growth looked impressive, but they were not backed up empirically.

Occasionally, there was anecdotal data. Anecdotes are easy to come by—you just read one of my own about learning lessons from pain in kindergarten. With hundreds of countries and numerous time-periods to choose from, one can cherry-pick data to support any theory. The last period in the U.S. that could be picked for that was from the late 1960s to the mid 1980s. This period is shown as the *right* part of the scatter plot in Figure 3-F, where growth improved by cutting the top tax rate from 70 percent to 50 percent. If it was true that a low top marginal rate improved growth, it would be true in the last thirty-four years (the *left* part of the scatter plot in 3-F or Figure 9-A).

It is not true.

Theory at Odds with Reality

It is hard for economists to understand a low top marginal tax rate is bad for growth when large consulting fees and salaries depend on theorizing a low top rate is good for growth. Note the best-fit line in Figure 9-A slopes upward. To earn those consulting fees and salaries, economists must theorize it slopes downward. CEOs, business owners, and owners of large stock portfolios who got most of the $21.8 trillion that didn't go to workers over the last forty-one years fund organizations such as the U.S. Chamber of

Commerce, the Heritage Foundation, the Cato Institute, the Tax Foundation, and others that pay economists to theorize low marginal tax rates are good for growth.

They also fund the politicians who promise to cut marginal tax rates. They are the favored target audience for the financial media. *The Wall Street Journal* and CNBC earn more advertising dollars by catering to what CEOs, business owners, and large-stock-portfolio owners want to believe.

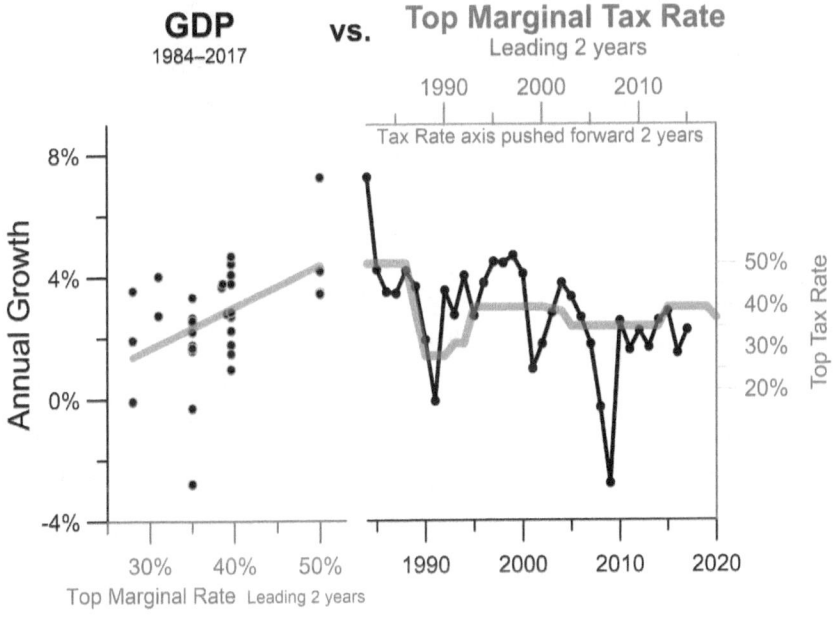

Figure 9-A

I don't believe there is some grand conspiracy here any more than I doubt Einstein's sincerity in opposing quantum mechanics or my own failed intention to use valuation to perform well for my clients. I just think most people have been educated into a box, while vital parts of reality lie outside that box. The humility to reconsider current beliefs paves a path for progress.

Further evidence the PhDs suffer with paradigm blindness: during each of the last eight years, the consensus GDP forecast was that growth would surge back at least to 3 percent in the next year; then, as the next year unfolded, they had to walk back the forecast to a growth rate closer to the tax-policy model I introduced in Chapter 3.

There are a few concepts that make the emperor's nakedness harder to see from inside the box. We already discussed in Chapter 2 that lower marginal tax rates on income up to about 2.5 times the average wage encourage workers to put in more hours. This small-pocket effect also improves the incentive to run a business. This concept appears legitimate, but not for the top marginal rate. Two more concepts that help enable staying in the box are *tax efficiency* and the *Laffer Curve*.

Tax Efficiency: The Wrong Goal

Martian Feldstein, who helped engineer the 1986 tax reform under Reagan, talks glowingly about tax efficiency, which measures how effectively a tax rate raises revenue. The reform was billed as revenue-neutral—it eliminated deductions, reduced the number of brackets to two, and cut the top bracket to the lowest in history. The top rate went from 50 to 28 percent while the capital-gains rate was raised to a matching 28 percent.

After the reform, people at the top of the income-spectrum reported enough income under the 28 percent marginal tax rate that they paid more tax than when their marginal rate was 50 percent. They also paid a higher share of the income tax. This would be impressive if their higher tax payments had been generated by faster economic growth—but it was not. As we have shown in Chapters 1 and 3, growth slowed with the 28 percent top rate.

Feldstein considers the higher 50 percent marginal rate as inefficient, since it raised less revenue from the wealthy; he calls this loss of collected revenue a "deadweight loss." I call it *putting money in the big pocket.* In the 1980s, some of what went into the big pocket was junk investment—but some of it was rocket fuel for growth.

Using the two-year lead time, during the five years influenced by the 50 percent top rate GDP grew at 4.5 percent. The three years influenced by the 28 percent top rate annualized 1.8 percent. Even though the wealthy were paying more tax, the growth rate of Federal revenue declined (as would be expected with a slower-growing economy).

If the goal is prosperity, we don't want the top rate to be efficient at raising revenue for the government; we want it to encourage plowing money into big pockets and growing businesses and the economy.

Bogus Laffer Curve

The idea of tax efficiency and the wealthy's tax payments surging with tax-cuts—even though the growth rate of all federal revenue declines—helps keep alive the idea of the Laffer Curve. This idea (developed by economist Arthur Laffer) points out that if a tax rate were zero percent, it would raise no revenue. As the tax rate rises, the amount of revenue also rises, up to the point that the tax rate becomes so high that revenue lost to tax-avoidance becomes larger than the increase in revenue from a higher tax rate. So in theory there is a tax rate that maximizes revenue, and that if the tax rate is above that optimal point you can increase revenue by cutting the tax rate. This is part of the inside-the-box thinking that completely ignores tax brackets.

If there were only one tax rate and every dollar of income were taxed at that rate, a Laffer Curve would probably be a reasonable tool. In a marginal-tax-rate system, it may just be a logical-sounding hypothetical with no basis in reality. Unlike all the curved best-fit lines you have seen in this book, where the best-fit plot is mathematically calculated from actual data, all the Laffer Curves I have seen are drawn hypothetically. I have never found one based on actual data.

I haven't even found one with units on an axis. On the x-axis for the tax rate, is it the average tax rate, the average marginal rate, the top marginal rate, or revenue as a share of GDP? No Laffer curve I have seen clarifies this distinction. What about the y-axis for revenue—is it measured in dollars, inflation-adjusted dollars, real dollars per capita, or revenue as a share of GDP? There is no specification.

Back in the 1990s when I experimented with trying to plot a Laffer Curve, I couldn't come up with anything reasonable. If I had made a Laffer Curve in 1942, an 81 percent top rate would have maximized revenue. In 1985, the then-current 50 percent rate would appear best. In 2005, the 35 percent rate would appear to maximize revenue. Even if such a curve were a real thing, the idea of maximizing tax revenue does not seem like a worthy goal—and certainly not a conservative goal. Yet, from inside of the box the Laffer Curve looks reasonable for anyone who just causally looks at the curve and listens to what the financial media says about it. And it is especially attractive for someone wanting to cut the top marginal tax rate.

Staying in the Box

Vagueness makes it easier to stay in the box. About ten years ago, I started paying close attention to anyone promoting the belief that a low top tax rate improved growth. I wanted to know precisely *when* they thought the top marginal tax rate influenced growth. You've read my claims several times now that the influence comes two years later. After ten years, I still have not found an economist or pundit who claims a low top rate promotes growth and also specifies when the influence should occur. My take on this is that if they specified a lead time it would be too easy to empirically show the claim was false.

For example, I once visited with a banker who, when asked about the lead time, speculated cutting the top rate this year would help growth next year—so a one-year lead time. If you test the data in Figure 9-A, the correlation with a one-year lead time is still positive, where a higher top rate corresponds with faster growth. While the correlation is not quite as strong as with the two-year lead, it is empirically false to claim that if the top rate is at 50 percent or below, cutting it correlates with faster growth.

The gatekeepers of the box, those 0.01 percent, also limit conflicting analysis. In the introduction to this book I mentioned I presented a paper at a Western Economic Association International (WEAI) conference in 2008. If you presented, you could submit the paper to one of the two WEAI journals without the usual submission fee. The journal's policy was to send a paper to two independent reviewers and within two months let the author know whether the paper would be published, published with revisions, or rejected.

About a year after submitting, I finally received word from one independent reviewer who had some useful comments and recommended publishing. (I have no idea if there was a second reviewer.) The editor of the journal apologized for the long delay and decided not to publish. A few other journals also rejected the piece.

For a while I chalked this up to not having the PhD credential. Then I read about the case of Daniel Holland as recounted by Dr. Robert H. Parks in his book *Unlocking the Secrets of Wall Street*.

The late Dr. Holland, a Professor Emeritus at MIT, was commissioned to do a $300,000 study in the late 1960s on the damaging effect the income tax had on the incentive of executives (today that would be about $2 million adjusted for inflation, or $3.7 million adjusted for GDP/p). The top tax rate at the time was 77 percent. The summary of the study concluded, "most executives—eighty percent of our sample—were apparently not deterred as regards the effort they devote to their main job by the income tax."

After spending the equivalent of several million dollars, the funders of the study refused to approve its publication anywhere. Why? It was not consistent with their inside-the-box view. Dr. Parks notes that, in addition to after-tax income, executives work for prestige, power, accomplishment, peer approval, and many other things. Perhaps in addition to generous salaries and consulting fees, getting published also requires promoting a theory that can't be supported empirically. The box tends to be self-reinforcing.

Misperception can remain for generations. At some point, false beliefs bring enough pain that people willingly change how they believe, act, or vote. Prosperity-restoring policy probably does not need to wait for people to die, as Plank's idea above suggests. If a small percentage of the voting public started consistently voting for prosperity, it would shift the political balance to enact better policy.

In this chapter, we described the prevailing views about a low top marginal tax rate being good for the economy as a box that economists, CEOs, the financial media, as well as the public, are educated into. We discussed how this box prevents seeing a reality outside and how the people in the box are most likely sincere in their beliefs. This brings up a problem for people in the box. They have to explain away bad economic results after they get the tax policy favored in the box.

The next chapter deals with their current favorite excuse.

Chapter 10
Wolf in Sheep's Clothing Uses the Fed as a Scapegoat

In this chapter, we will see the wolf—those who get the short-term benefit from a low top tax rate—is fooled by the sheepskin it wears, as pointed out in the last chapter. The wolf is unaware that it is the problem behind slow growth. Not only does the wolf deny its part, but it points the finger at the Federal Reserve and actually has many believing the Fed is the problem.

We will look at the history of inflation and monetary policy. While acknowledging the Fed has made mistakes, we will make a case that we are better off with the Fed the last hundred years and that it has done a good job the last ten years.

The wolf doesn't know it's a wolf. The people who got the $21.8 trillion instead of it going to workers (mentioned in Chapter 1) think they're protecting freedom and the system that created the greatest prosperity the world has known. "Protector of prosperity" is the sheep's skin they hide under as they advocate the low marginal tax rates that reduce wealth creation.

I need to be careful here. Let me clarify: claiming the ultra-wealthy hide under a sheep's skin does not mean I think they are less moral than the rest of us or that their state of denial is any greater. If anyone else were in their shoes, they would probably have the same beliefs. Besides, when it comes to creating widespread prosperity that grows the pie for all, we will be dependent on those "wolves."

The wolves are not willing to admit the low marginal tax rates they struggled so mightily to obtain are an influence behind weak growth, a declining middle class, asset bubbles, trade and budget deficits, and America's declining place in the world. They dismiss calls for higher marginal tax rates as "class warfare."

This may be a case of what the Apostle Paul says in Romans 2:1: "When you accuse another, you condemn yourself." As Warren Buffett quips, "We have already had class warfare and my class won." The share of wealth and income has shifted to the top while growth has slowed, which meets our definition of "class warfare."

So far, elites have used scapegoats to keep the middle class from blaming them for their shrinking share of the pie and stagnant or shrinking standard of living. The scapegoats include the Federal Reserve Bank (or "the Fed"), regulations, the "lazy poor who don't pull their weight," China, Mexico, immigrants who "steal their jobs," or world trade and technology which "drive down wages."

The wolves have done an effective job of blaming the Fed. In my conversations about the economy over the last several years, several people expressed shock that I didn't also blame the Fed for the slow growth, the bubbles, and the dismal income for savers. A substantial market exists for blogs and books peddling and feeding this belief. A current example is *FED Up*, which blames the Fed for the slow growth and "callously" slashing interest income for retirees to benefit the big banks.

As Chapter 8 pointed out, these problems likely stem from bad tax policy rather than the Fed. Low real interest rates are *normal* with slow economic growth. What we call the "real interest rate" is the actual interest rate minus the rate of inflation. When growth is weak, the real interest rate tends to be low or even negative, which means inflation is higher than the interest rate. Actually, weakness tends to show up in real interest rates a few months *before* it shows up in GDP growth.

The Fed is often blamed for destroying the purchasing power of the dollar. There is validity to the claim, but this may not have harmed our wellbeing after all. Figure 10-A shows the consumer price index was very volatile from 1750 to 1913 (when the Fed was created). There were rapid movements up and down in prices—especially around wars—but the price index did not trend up over the long span. Since creation of the Fed in 1913, purchasing power of the dollar has declined.

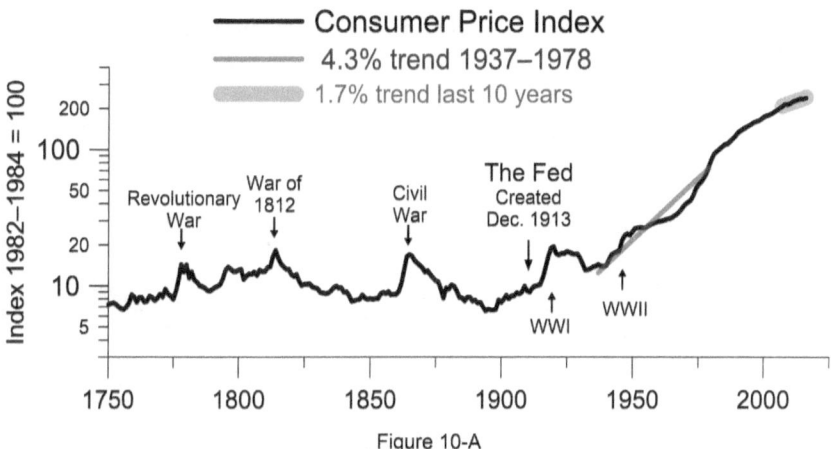

Figure 10-A

However, our economic well-being is determined by growth in the standard of living, not by a change in prices. While the overall rate of GDP growth was probably faster prior to the Fed, the rate of growth per person has probably been faster since the Fed's beginning in 1913. I say *probably* here because I am less certain of data prior to 1929; it is not currently considered official data. The preponderance of the data, however, suggests the improvement of individual lives has been better since the Fed was created.

If we could eliminate the bad tax policy that led to weak periods of growth in the last ninety-eight years, growth in standard of living would likely be much better going forward than it was prior to the Fed.

The Fed is sometimes blamed for letting the Great Depression get so deep. They certainly could have done more to prevent deflation. One of the Fed's takeaways from the forty-three-month recession that took us to the bottom of the Depression was to not allow significant deflation. While deflation following World War I did not take prices down to previous lows, prices still fell 40 percent from the 1920-high. Almost three-quarters of the drop was between 1929 and 1933.

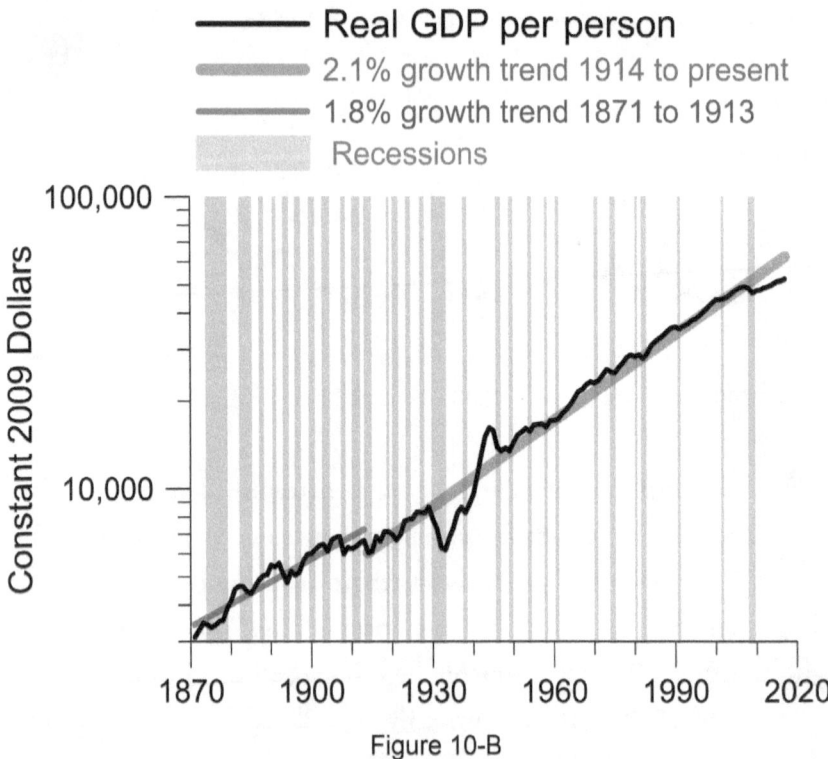

Figure 10-B

From the pain of those times, the Fed developed an institutional conviction to not allow significant deflation. When the next test came with the 1937-38 recession, deflation was held to a modest amount. From 1937 to the time of the Humphrey Hawkins Legislation in 1978, inflation trended higher at a 4.3 percent pace. Instead of periods of high inflation interspersed with deflation, we had periods of high inflation interspersed with *low* inflation. While a 4.3 percent pace cuts the purchasing power of a dollar in half every 16.5 years, it was still not as destructive as deflation would have been.

Recessions became less frequent and shorter with the Fed's conviction to vigorously fight deflation, along with some aspects of FDR's New Deal such as bank deposit insurance and unemployment compensation. Prior to March 1933, the economy was in recession about 48 percent of the time. Since then we have been in recession just under 15 percent of the time. So instead of scapegoating the Fed, we may want to thank the Fed.

In my first economics course at Vanderbilt, Dr. Shahan speculated that growth would be strongest with about a 1 percent rate of inflation. Several years ago I set out to see what that relationship really was. After much experimenting, the most meaningful correlation came from looking at the seven-year GDP growth rate compared to the six-year rate of inflation leading one year. Using the six-year inflation rate had just as strong a correlation as the seven-year rate and gave a full year of lead time.

I like lead times.

Figure 10-C suggests an inflation rate of 0.6 percent brings the strongest growth. However, that 0.6 percent is close to a cliff: deflation appears to be about seven times harder on growth than inflation. So the optimal range of inflation for growth would be between 0.3 and 3 percent.

Several central banks, including the Fed, aim for about 2 percent inflation. Often a recession will take inflation *down* 2 percent. So, if inflation were running at 1 percent and a recession hit, the rate could easily drop to minus-1 percent. Such deflation could potentially spiral a downturn much deeper. With a 2 percent rate of inflation, a central bank has a chance to stave off deflation when a

Put Money in Your Pocket | 129

recession hits. It's kind of like the view from a cliff; the best view is right up close, but you don't want to live on the edge in case you stumble or there's a strong gust of wind.

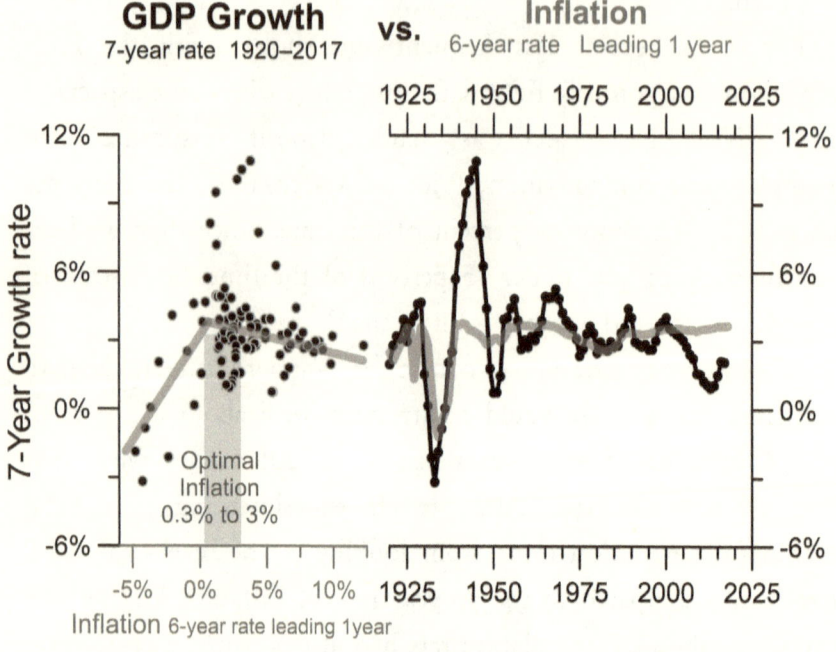

Figure 10-C

Inflation annualizing 1.7 percent the last seven years puts monetary policy about as close to optimizing growth as it has ever been. The growth model from Chapter 3 estimated GDP would grow at 1.5 percent the last seven years, but it actually grew at 2.1. Good monetary policy may well be the reason it was stronger.

During the great recession and financial crisis, the Fed's huge intervention probably staved off deflation and may have helped prevent the crisis from being much worse. Figure 10-D shows that the monetary base quadrupled—even as currency in circulation (the green stuff and coins) grew at roughly a normal historical rate. The broader measure of money, M2, also grew at close to its average rate of about 5.5 percent. People looking at the monetary base or the Fed balance sheet (in true Chicken Little-fashion) who warned of hyper inflation turned out to be wrong.

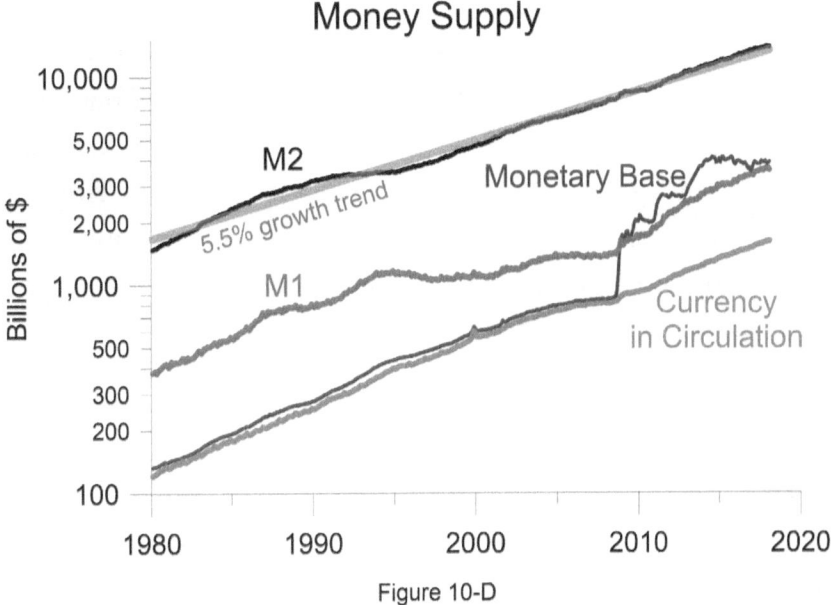

Figure 10-D

The Fed's job from 2007 through 2017 was at least competent and perhaps extraordinary in keeping inflation near the ideal range.

Using the Fed as a scapegoat invites politicians to intervene, which only risks more trouble. When politicians have leverage over a central bank, bad things are more likely to happen. You've probably heard about hyper inflation in Brazil or in the German Weimar Republic where inflation in a couple of years reduced the equivalent of several million dollars to less value than a postage stamp. During that period, most German government-spending came from borrowing money or printing it. Only a small percentage was raised in taxes.

Politicians are driven by the next election. Getting money spent in your district or state helps reelect congressmen and senators. So does cutting taxes. The combined incentive tends to run up deficits. If such politicians also have the power to print money or too much leverage over the central bank that has that power, it becomes dangerous.

The closest the U.S. comes to printing money to cover government expenses in our system is when the Fed monetizes the debt, which means it buys Treasury bonds directly from the Treasury. This is what "quantitative easing" did. It's helped drive up the Fed balance sheet and monetary base. If the Fed were free of political pressure, it would probably only monetize debt when necessary to prevent deflation or if it were considered beneficial to both high employment and stable prices.

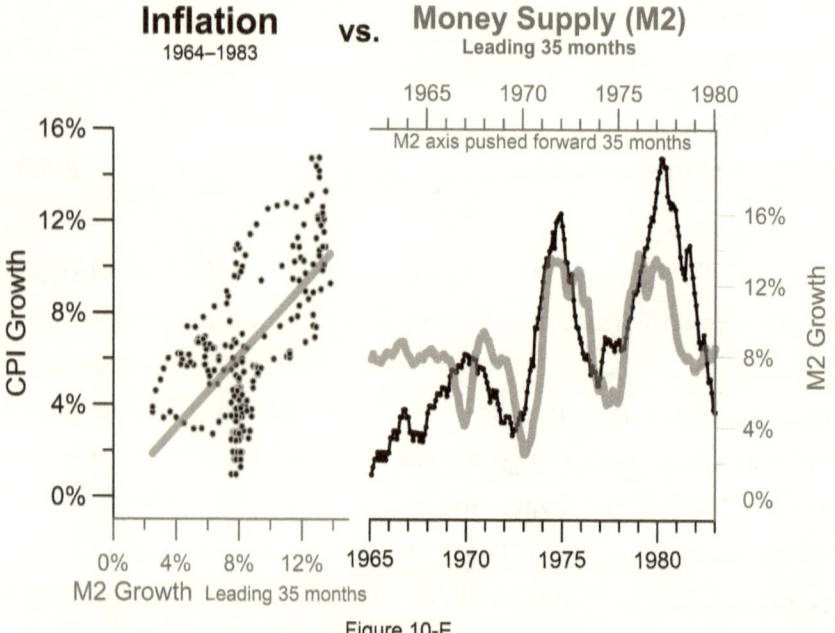

Figure 10-E

Political pressure on the Fed was easier before the 1978 Humphrey Hawkins legislation, which changed the Fed's mandate to include stable prices, made it more transparent, and required it to testify before Congress twice a year to explain its policy aims and the actions it took to achieve them. In the two Presidential elections before Humphrey Hawkins, pressure appears to have been applied to the Fed.

A colleague of mine in Thomasville, Georgia—Ron Salter—once told me about a conversation he had with John Ehrlichman. They got to talking about economics and Ron said he thought Presidents got the kind of monetary policy they wanted. Ehrlichman replied, "That was certainly true in the Nixon era." He related how Fed Chairman Arthur Burns would answer, "Yes sir, Mr. President." Ehrlichman wasn't sure why President Nixon picked him to sit in on all the meetings with the Fed Chairman. He remembered feeling sorry for the professorial old gentleman with his Meerschaum pipe. The data is consistent with that having happened.

There were two times in the 1970s when the growth rate of money as measured by M2 went to double digits. The first was during Nixon's reelection campaign of 1972, and the second was during Ford's 1976 campaign. Chairman Burns presided over both of them. About thirty-five months after the bouts of double-digit money growth, we had double-digit inflation, which peaked in 1975 and 1980.

Leading into President Jimmy Carter's run for reelection, the new Fed Chairman Paul Volcker, with greater independence than his predecessor and a legal mandate to pursue stable prices, began hiking interest rates to restrain money growth and inflation. He kept hiking them until a recession started in January of 1980.

When the Fed's primary mandate was "full employment," monetary policy usually tried to keep interest rates low and stable. Implementing the new dual mandate contributed to the highest interest rates since at least the Civil War in the mid-nineteenth century. The current mandate appears to be working; since January 1980, the long-term rate of inflation has trended closer and closer to the level that likely best supports a strong economy.

The changes in monetary policy appear to have changed the relationship between money growth and inflation: since 1983, the correlation is weaker than in Figure 10-E and appears to have a sixty-one-month lead time rather than the thirty-five-month lead shown in this graph.

While I don't know for sure, I like to think Carter knew giving up influence over the Fed and creating the broader mandate would harm his reelection bid and did it anyway for the good of the country. His post-Presidential work supports this plausibility. At the time I thought Carter was a poor President and didn't vote for him, but now I believe he's quite underrated.

Any action to give elected politicians more influence over the Fed likely risks worse economic outcomes.

In this chapter we saw the most growth-friendly rate of inflation is probably between about 0.3 and 3 percent. Erring on the low side and risking deflation is seven times more dangerous than erring on the high side.

We made a case that our standard of living has improved at a faster pace since the Fed was created in 1913, and we have noted the Fed has gotten better over time. It did a poor job prior to 1933, but likely helped reduce recessions by two-thirds since. We speculated that good monetary policy offset some of the harm from destructive tax policy in recent years. We also warned of the dangers of giving politicians influence over monetary policy.

In the next chapter we look at three Republican Presidents who rescued the economy from recession with tax increases.

Chapter 11
Hoover the Hero

We have just looked at how the wolf blames others to hide the destructive influence of low marginal tax rates from themselves and the public.

Here we look at more information the wolf does not want known.

Three Republican Presidents—Herbert Hoover, Ronald Reagan, and George H. W. Bush—rescued the economy from recession with tax increases. I am pretty sure you have never seen anyone else lay out the facts as I am about to. When they are laid out in sequential order, the facts stack up to this conclusion. We'll also look at how FDR put in the best tax policy ever, but followed it up with the second-worst tax-policy blunder behind that which led to the Great Depression.

You may ask, Haven't I heard the pundits left and right blame Hoover for the Great Depression? How he kicked it off with raising tariffs? And how after he raised income taxes the Depression lasted eight more years? Sure, I've heard all those claims. And then, if I didn't already have the data, I would download it into my database and analyze it.

Smoot Hawley Tariffs Didn't Cause Depression

First let's dispatch with the Smoot Hawley tariffs as a cause of the Depression. The tariffs enacted in 1930 continued till after World War II. If they were so devastating, how come they also allowed 11 percent GDP growth in 1934, or 13 percent in 1936, or the 19 percent growth in 1942?

Net exports declined from 0.3 percent of GDP in 1929 to 0.2 percent of GDP in 1933—hardly capable of explaining the 27 percent drop in GDP (45 percent drop if you don't account for deflation). Sure, trade declined, but only about as much as GDP itself. Plus, the first recession of the Depression started in September of 1929 nine months before the tariffs were enacted.

Now that we have that out of the way, let's tackle that income tax increase where in June 1932 the top bracket went from 25 percent on income above $100,000 to 63 percent on income above a million dollars. It's important here to distinguish between the part of the Depression where we were plummeting to the bottom and the part in which we were rapidly recovering.

Recovery Began with Hoover's Tax Increase

In the eleven months after Hoover's tax increase, almost everything started improving. The stock market hit bottom on July 8 and ended higher in July than in June when taxes went up. A year later it was up over 120 percent. Industrial production hit its low in July 1932. It was weaker than any time since the index began in 1919—but rose 119 percent to a new high in 1936 and trended even higher until the next recession.

Two recessions occurred in the Great Depression. The forty-three-month one that took us to the bottom officially ended in March 1933. The unemployment rate hit its worst level in May 1933. A year after Hoover's big tax increase, virtually everything was improving.

The 63 percent rate on income above a million dollars enacted in 1932 changed behavior. In 1931, seventy-seven individual tax returns reported income over $1 million. In 1932 that dropped to twenty tax returns. It is not as if these people disappeared, but with the higher tax rate they built their businesses rather than taking income.

After the two-year lag, GDP grew almost 11 percent in 1934 and annualized that 11 percent growth for three years through 1936. New all-time highs were set in 1936 for GDP, industrial production, and a total real return stock index shown in figure 8-D back in Chapter 8. The expansion lasted fifty months—the longest ever at the time.

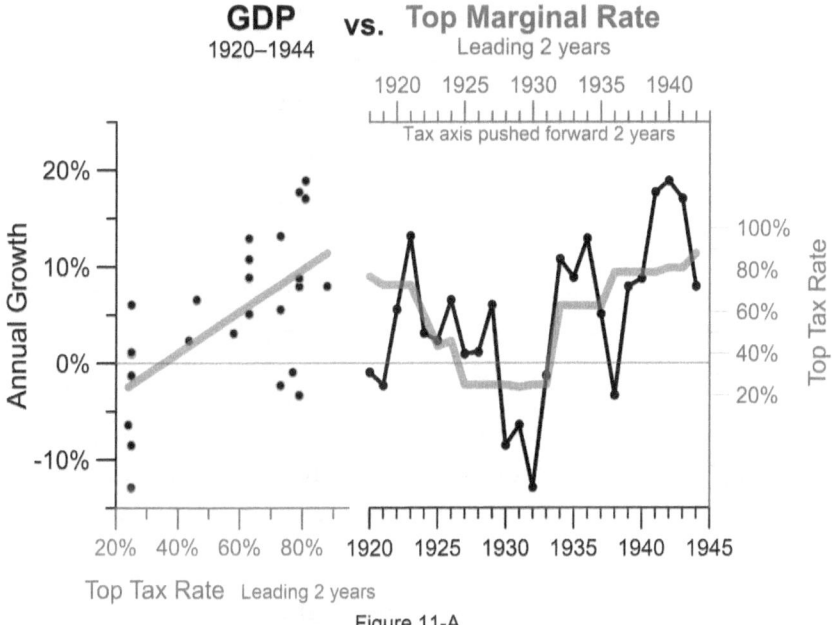

Figure 11-A

Hoover didn't raise taxes with the expectation it would launch the longest and strongest recovery-expansion in the US up to that time. There was no theory to support that. He raised them with the intent of avoiding an even bigger crisis.

Prevailing economic thought then was that a large budget deficit risked collapsing the currency and potentially unleashing hyperinflation like the Weimer Republic in Germany.

Hoover began pushing for a tax increase when the fiscal year ending June 1931 ended in a deficit. Federal revenues would decline

50 percent in the next fiscal year. Democrats who were newly in charge of Congress after being out for a decade resisted such an unpopular move. The issue came to a head when a run on the dollar got out of hand. We were on the gold standard at the time. During the month of May, 1932 foreign nations redeemed nearly $200 million for gold. Congress passed the tax increase the next month.

Hoover acted to protect the nation. As one of the wealthiest men in the country the tax increase hit him particularly hard. He and his party took most of the brunt for the unpopular increase. Self sacrifice with the intention to serve the nation that results in monumental recovery is heroic by any standard.

Despite full recovery of GDP 1936 was not the end of the Depression. Nonfarm jobs didn't recover until 1940 and the total number of jobs may not have recovered until early 1942. Jobs took longer to recover because the lead time for the tax-increase to influence the labor market is longer and productivity grew rapidly. Anyone who has read or watched Steinbeck's *The Grapes of Wrath* has a vivid image of tractors displacing lots of farm workers.

On top of this, a sharp thirteen-month recession ending in mid-1938 set back the recovery. Unemployment—which had been cut by more than half—surged, but no indicator approached the worst levels set in 1932 and 1933. Strong GDP growth before and after this second recession meant every five-year period that included this downturn annualized growing at least 6 percent a year, about four-and-a-quarter times faster than the ten years ending in 2017.

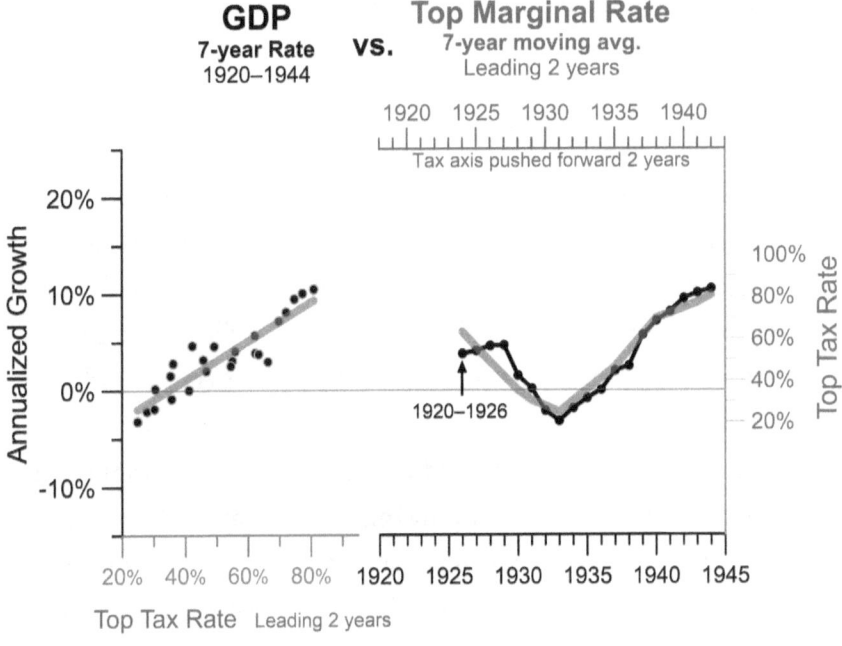

Figure 11-B

The top tax rate and growth had a strong correlation in this period, however in Figure 11-A, annual fluctuations in the growth rate make the actual relationship harder to see. We can fix this by looking at the seven-year growth rate compared with the seven-year moving-average of the top marginal rate. This also smoothes out much of the effect of the business cycle and allows us to see the long-term influence of the top rate. Figure 11-B likely overstates the correlation between the top rate and growth, in that it is sometimes easier to get a good fit with shorter periods of data, but it is very consistent with the lead time and relationship of analyzing the last ninety-eight years.

Hoover and his tax-increase launched the recovery for which FDR got most of the credit. The seven years influenced by the 25 percent top rate that President Calvin Coolidge put into place annualized shrinking GDP at 3.2 percent. It was the worst seven-year

U.S. GDP growth rate ever. In this book, Coolidge is the culprit in the Great Depression and Hoover is the hero.

FDR: Best Tax Policy Ever

FDR became President in March 1933. The 20th Ammendment to the Constitution moving inauguration to January 20 was ratified under Hoover on January 23, 1933 too late for FDR's first inauguration. He was in office about twelve years. The economy was in recession during his first month and for thirteen months in 1937-38. Those fourteen months were the only months of recession under FDR. Rapid growth prevailed during the other 144 months of his Presidency. GDP annualized growing 9.1 percent while he was in office. This rate dwarfs the results of any other President. However, it was greatly aided by Hoover, by the very low base from which growth started, and by World War II.

We have all been conditioned to believe World War II was the main part of the outperformance. My view of tax policy, however, creates some doubts about the extent of the war's influence. The best growth corresponds with FDR creating a $5 million top tax bracket. It was in place for six years: a 79 percent marginal rate was in place for four of the years and an 81 percent rate the last two. Using the three-year lead time for the top bracket we introduced in Chapter 3, growth annualized 13 percent with the $5 million bracket.

A 79- or 81 percent top rate sounds like it would have soaked the rich, but it didn't. Those rates hardly raised any Federal Revenue. I went to the IRS website and looked up the "Statistics of Income Report, Part 1" (SOI) for the years 1919-49. All the SOIs showed how many returns had $1 million of income or more. Six of them specified if tax returns had $5 million or more.

In 1938, three returns showed $5 million or more. The SOI for 1939 showed zero returns with $5 million. The SOI for the other years with a top bracket of $5 million did not report whether there were any tax returns with more than $5 million. For all I know, only three people ever paid at the 79 percent rate, and no one ever paid the 81 percent rate. There could have been a few, but the 13 percent GDP growth rate for those six years suggests the people who had the potential to take that much income were all busy building up value in their businesses instead.

FDR's Attempt to Soak Rich Kills Economy

After the $5 million bracket, which appears to be the most pro-growth tax policy in U.S. history, FDR made what I believe to be the second-worst tax policy blunder after Coolidge.

Roosevelt was gravely concerned about inflation. W.W.II, as previous wars, shrunk the supply of consumer goods and drove prices higher. Inflation hit double-digits in 1941 and was accelerating in early 1942. FDR was concerned the wealthy would bid the price of necessities beyond the reach of ordinary Americans.

He believed the way to assure all Americans could get enough to survive was to heavily tax the wealthy, impose price controls and ration numerous necessities.

In 1942, FDR cut the top bracket 96 percent, to $200,000, while raising the top rate to 88 percent. Two years later, he raised the top rate to 94 percent.

The policy did bring the rate of inflation down to low single digits in 1944, but... Remember the story of Reagan and the 94 percent tax rate from Chapter 2? In addition to discouraging work, heavy taxes discouraged business owners as well.

After the two year lag for the top rate going to 88 percent growth dropped to 8 percent in 1944 from the 17 percent the year before. After the three year lag for cutting the bracket the economy shrunk. Federal spending went up 5.9 percent in 1945 to its highest level of the war, yet the economy shrank 1 percent.

This $200,000 bracket started out at 206 times GDP/p, but shrunk with inflation and economic growth to 115 times. While the bracket might have been fine with a marginal rate below 60 percent, it corresponded with the worst growth outside the Great Depression.

After the two year lag for the 94 percent top rate, GDP declined 11.6 percent in 1946. To add a bit of context, Federal spending dropped from about 31 percent of GDP in 1945 to about 19.5 percent in 1946. The private sector did not shrink much that year, but did not pick up the slack until marginal rates were cut and the tax bracket increased.

Heavy tax on the wealthy using high tax rates at low brackets contributed to a shrinking economy in 1945, 1946, 1947 and 1949.

Now on to Ronald Reagan and George H. W. Bush, the other two Republican Presidents who pulled the economy out of recession with tax increases. Or, at least, the economy and financial markets responded strongly *after* tax increases.

Economy Booms with Reagan Tax *Increase*

To mention Reagan and tax increases in the same sentence sounds strange given the financial media has elevated Reagan tax-cuts to near mythological importance. Putting facts in the proper sequential order will help give a clearer picture.

Reagan correctly recognized that the 70 percent marginal tax rate was vastly too high for its bracket. He correctly noted that inflation had deflated the value of the bracket by about 60 percent. This understates the devaluation: using GDP/p, it was closer to 70 percent.

Reagan's big tax-cut became law in August 1981. The 1981–82 recession also began that month (although it was not officially labeled a "recession" until more than a year later). Robert H. Parks, who wrote *Unlocking the Secrets of Wall Street*, was one of the few economists who predicted that recession; he made the call in July 1981 based in part on the Reagan tax-cut he expected to come the next month. In the year after Reagan's big tax-cut, the stock market lost about 20 percent of its value. The unemployment rate which had ticked down to 7.2 percent in Reagan's first few months had risen to 9.8 percent, on its way to 10.8. The budget deficit was exploding. Reagan was pushing a tax increase through Congress which would take back a significant portion of his tax-cut, but would also leave the top rate at the reduced 50 percent. Given the low tax brackets, a 50 percent top rate was much closer to the growth-optimizing top rate than the 70 percent rate had been.

His tax increase, called the Tax Equity and Fiscal Responsibility Act (TEFRA), cleared the conference committee between the House and Senate working out their differences on Friday, August 13, 1982. This was the first up-day for stocks in the powerful "bull" market of the 1980s. The low of the "bear" market had been the day before. The market also soared when the House and Senate passed TEFRA and when Reagan signed it into law on September 3, 1982. The recession ended two months later and a powerful recovery and expansion began in December 1982. A year after the tax-increase, stocks were up about 62 percent and the economy was soaring. After the expansion peaked, it was the second-longest in history—or, as Republicans called it at the time, the "longest peace-time expansion ever."

TEFRA was a big increase. A few years later economists would argue about whether this or Clinton's increase was the biggest tax-hike in history. (We'll talk about Reagan cutting the top rate to 28 percent in Chapter 13.)

"Deal *(Crime)* of the Century" Ends Recession

George H. W. Bush also faced a recession that had begun in August 1990. He too saw falling stock prices and an exploding deficit. He was working on a budget deal to cut spending and increase taxes. Negotiations were likely going on as the stock market hit its low point on October 11, 1990. In his budget agreement address on October 25, he called it the "Deal of the Century." Some pundits opposed to any tax increase called it the "Crime of the Century." This increase took the top rate from 28 to 31 percent in January 1991. The recession ended two months later in March. The increase helped launch one of the most powerful bull markets in stocks ever and what is still the longest expansion in U.S. history.

The economy has too many moving parts to claim tax increases caused recessions to end and expansions to begin. However, the experiences of Hoover, Reagan, and Bush (41) suggest financial markets and the economy respond positively to leaders making unpopular, but responsible, decisions to raise taxes in times of large budget deficits. By "responsible tax increases," I mean moving marginal tax rates closer to their growth-optimizing level.

Above we recounted three Republican Presidents experiencing large budget deficits during an economic downturn. They all raised taxes and, roughly simultaneously, bear market stock declines ended and powerful bull markets began. Within a few months the economy also turned from decline to powerful, long expansion.

We also saw that FDR had great success with the highest tax bracket ever, but dismal results followed, trying to soak the rich by pairing high tax rates with low tax brackets. In the next chapter we try to piece all the information together to make the most pro-growth tax plan possible.

Chapter 12
Actual "Pro-Growth" Tax Policy

> *A good tree cannot bear bad fruit, neither can a bad tree bear good fruit. Every tree which does not bear good fruit will be cut down and cast into the fire. Thus by their fruit you will know them.* —Matthew 7:18-20.

When it comes to the tree of tax policy, hopefully the first eleven chapters have convinced you that what the wolf calls "pro-growth" tax policy—a top marginal rate below 38 percent and a capital-gains rate below 20 percent—bears bad fruit. In this chapter we will try to coax out of the limited data the marginal tax rate and bracket combinations that create the best incentives to work, run businesses, and grow the economy.

The suggested income-tax schedule below attempts to balance incentives for the little pocket and big pocket. We want a low average tax rate to encourage *running* businesses and high marginal rates to encourage avoiding taxes by *growing* them.

The tax schedule proposed below would have lowered the average tax rate for about 97 percent of tax payers from what they would have paid without the Trump tax cut. Unlike the Trump cut this cut would be permanent for individuals. However, faster growth from the proposed policy should mean people have more income and pay more tax—even at the lower tax rate. We will also look at three additional points that could make a big difference to growth.

In Chapter 3, we talked about the 50 percent top marginal rate corresponding with the best single year of growth in the last sixty-five years; but then, in Chapter 8, we showed its bracket was low and exposed the reader to the unhelpful effects of tax shelters disguised as investments. Here, we will now try to answer the question, What is the tax bracket that will optimize growth for a given marginal tax rate? This is part of trying to map the path for the most pro-growth income tax schedule.

Since I have found no one else asking these questions and can't find anything in the economic literature on how the level of tax brackets influences growth, I hereby proclaim myself the world's leading expert on this subject. After all, I have been pondering this issue for over a decade. I will willingly defer this title when more-credentialed economists take up the question. Indeed, the purpose of this book will be partly achieved when that happens.

A Deeper Look at Marginal Tax Rate's Impact on Growth

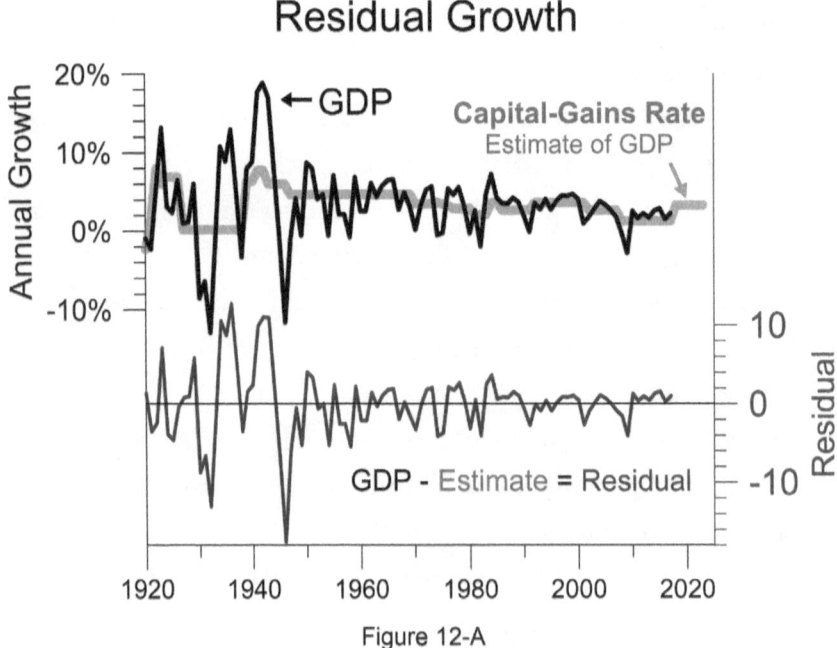

Figure 12-A

In pursuing the growth effect of a marginal tax rate, I want to isolate its influence from other influences on growth. For example, I don't want the effect of the capital-gains tax rate to mask how the top rate influences growth. So to take that effect out, I will start with GDP growth and then subtract the influence of the capital-gains rate we estimated in Chapter 3. This is shown in Figure 12-A. The difference shown in the bottom part of the chart is the residual, or the "error terms." It is the part of growth that the capital-gains rate did not estimate.

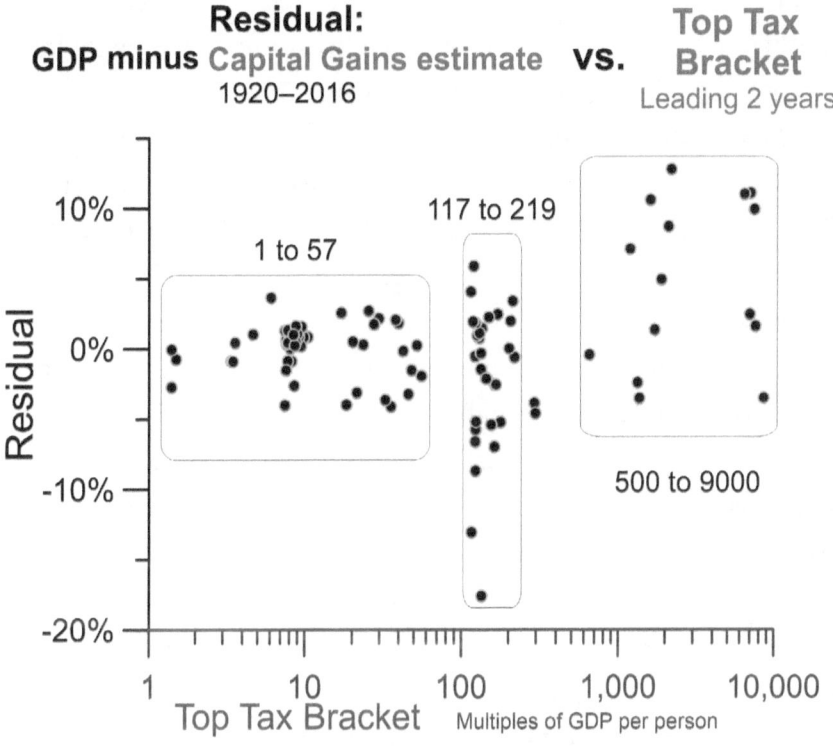

Figure 12-B

To control for the bracket, I looked at the residual growth from Figure 12-A within three ranges of the bracket. Figure 12-B shows the ranges within rectangles: the first rectangle shows residual growth when the top bracket was between 1 and 57 times GDP/p; the second rectangle shows the range from 117 to 219; the third shows the range above 649 times.

Put Money in Your Pocket | 147

There are two data points with a bracket between 292 and 297 times that did not make it into a rectangle. This does not mean they were not examined. I experimented extensively, adding or excluding points on the edge of each group. With limited data, sometimes the inclusion of just one point implied vastly different conclusions. If I were trying to "torture the data" to support a preconceived conclusion, choosing which points to include in a group would probably be the best way to do it. I have tried to include the points in each group which gives the clearest picture of reality.

When it comes to understanding how torturing the data works, I leaned from the best. In the 1980s I used to religiously read editorials in *The Wall Street Journal* about policies that made the economy strong or weak. Once I memorized the beginning and ending dates of recessions, it was easy to spot bias.

To paint some policy or another in favorable terms, the period under review would begin roughly at the end of a recession and end near the top of an expansion. Such editorials were kind of like comparing one person's hourly productivity during a work day to another's hourly productivity during a twenty-four-hour day—or, even worse, while they were asleep. While there were some liberal-leaning editorials, a large majority favored conservatives, Republicans, and low taxes.

Hopefully it's clear my agenda is not self-serving, although I would handily fit into the 97 percent that I am proposing tax-cuts for.

Each data-group in Figure 12-B has been controlled for the effect of capital gains and partially for the top bracket, since the influence is within a range. Figures 12-C through 12-E are scatter plots which will hopefully give three growth-optimizing tax rates for the three ranges of income.

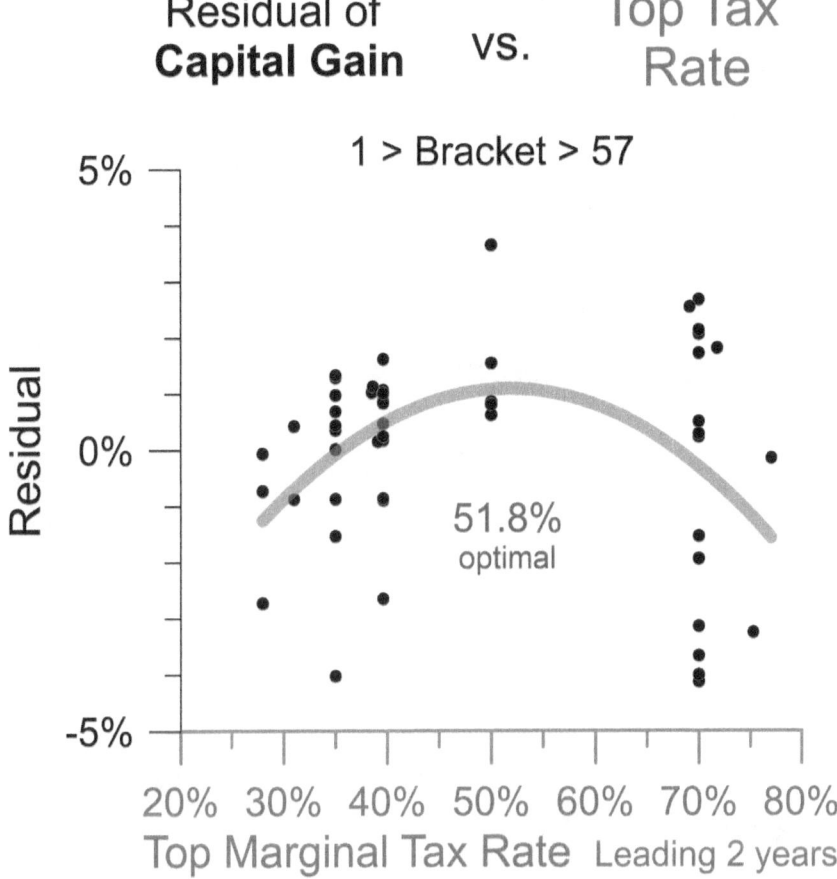

Figure 12-C

The data in the first rectangle is plotted with the top tax rate in Figure 12-C. The best-fit curve suggests the growth-optimizing top marginal rate is 51.8 percent (in Chapter 3 we called the data in this bracket-range the "Low Bracket era"). The best-fit curve to growth there suggested a rate of 54.5 percent would maximize growth. Controlling for the influence of capital gains probably makes the conclusion of 51.8 percent more accurate.

What was referred to as the "high bracket" data in Chapter 3 has been split into two groups. Figure 12-D shows the lower-bracket part of the split and suggests a 58.4 percent top rate maximizes growth. If we had included the next point or two (which are not included in a group, as explained above), it would suggest a 61 percent top rate optimized growth. Wrestling with this data for the last ten years made that higher rate feel less accurate.

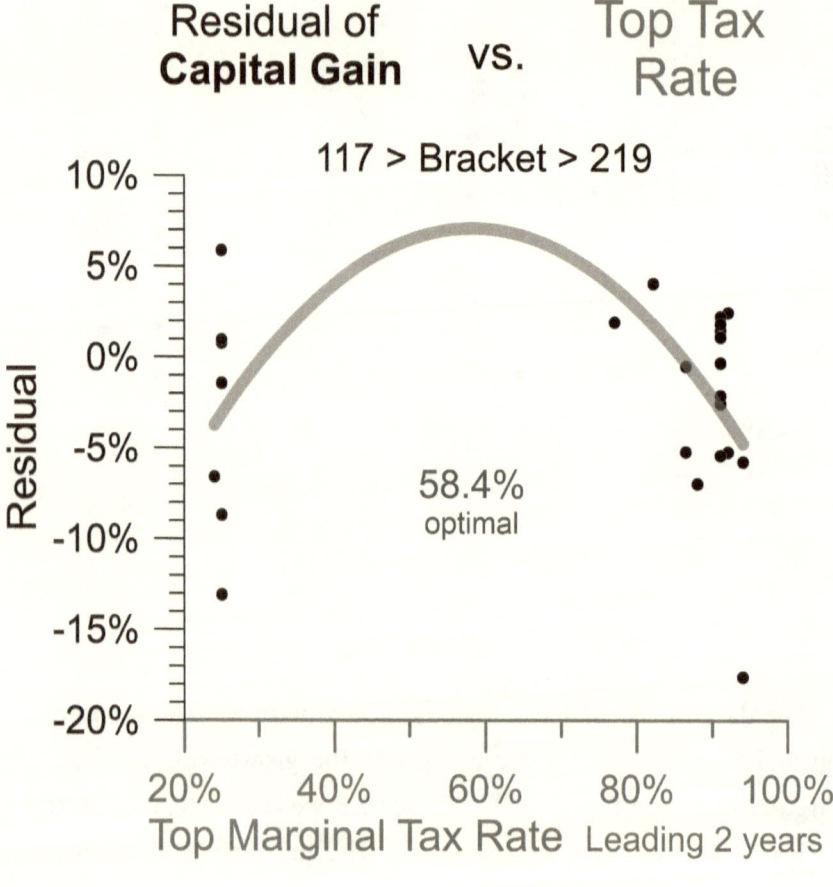

Figure 12-D

The highest-bracket data (third rectangle) suggests a top rate of 65.8 percent would bring the best growth. The strongest residual growth came with Hoover's 63 percent top marginal rate. This is a contrast to actual growth, where FDR's 79- to 81 percent top rates had the strongest growth.

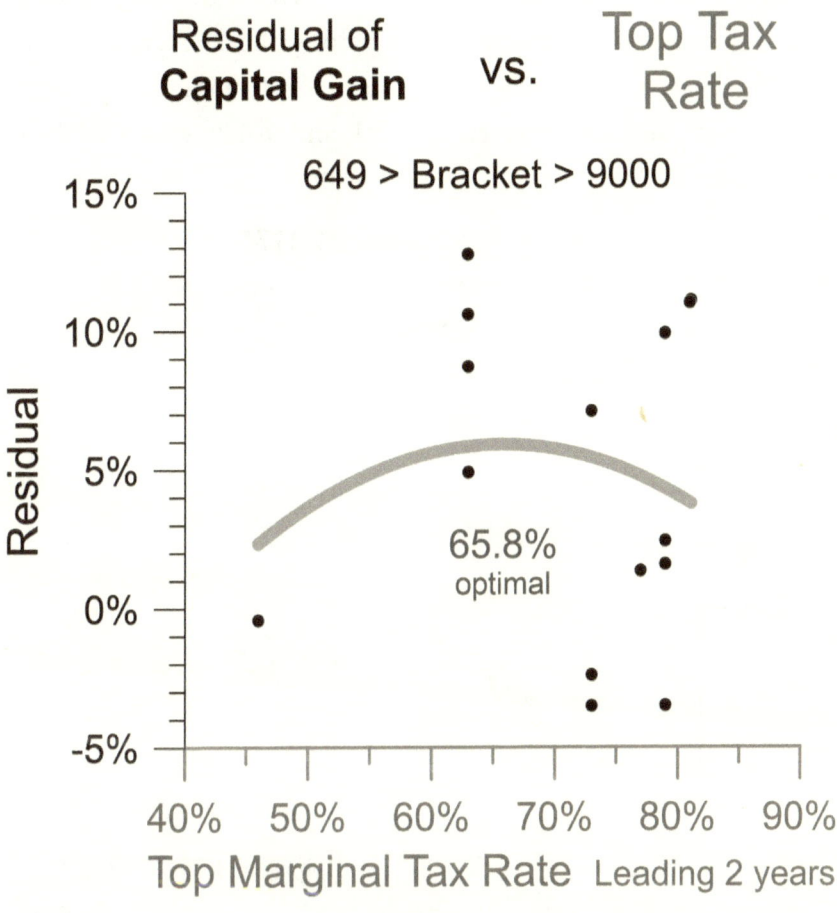

Figure 12-E

Figure 12-E had the least data to work with and was the most sensitive to which points I included. I could have supported a top tax rate as high as 72 percent or as low as 63 percent. However, I believe that 65.8 percent is the best guess for the growth-optimizing rate.

The next task is to pick optimal brackets for the three marginal tax rates identified in the last three figures. Given the evidence that high brackets are better for growth, instead of using the middle of the range, I believe a bracket at about 75 percent of the range would be better for growth. Therefore, I am pairing the 51.8 percent rate with a bracket of 43 times GDP/p. The 58.4- and 65.8 percent marginal tax rates get brackets of 194 and 6,600 times GDP/p (respectively).

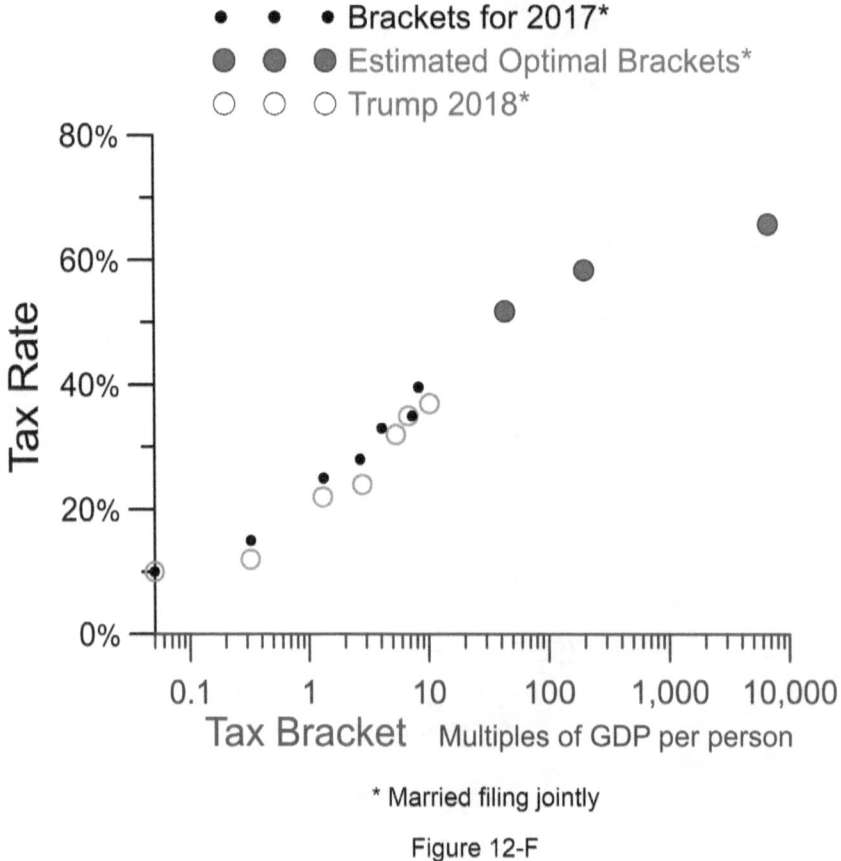

* Married filing jointly

Figure 12-F

If I have done the work correctly (and again, as the world's leading expert on this subject, I believe I have), the larger gray dots in Figure 12-F suggest the most pro-growth path for tax brackets: the path that strikes the ideal balance between a low-enough average tax rate to encourage running a business and a high-enough marginal rate to encourage avoiding taxes by growing the business. Or I could say balancing the small pocket and big pocket.

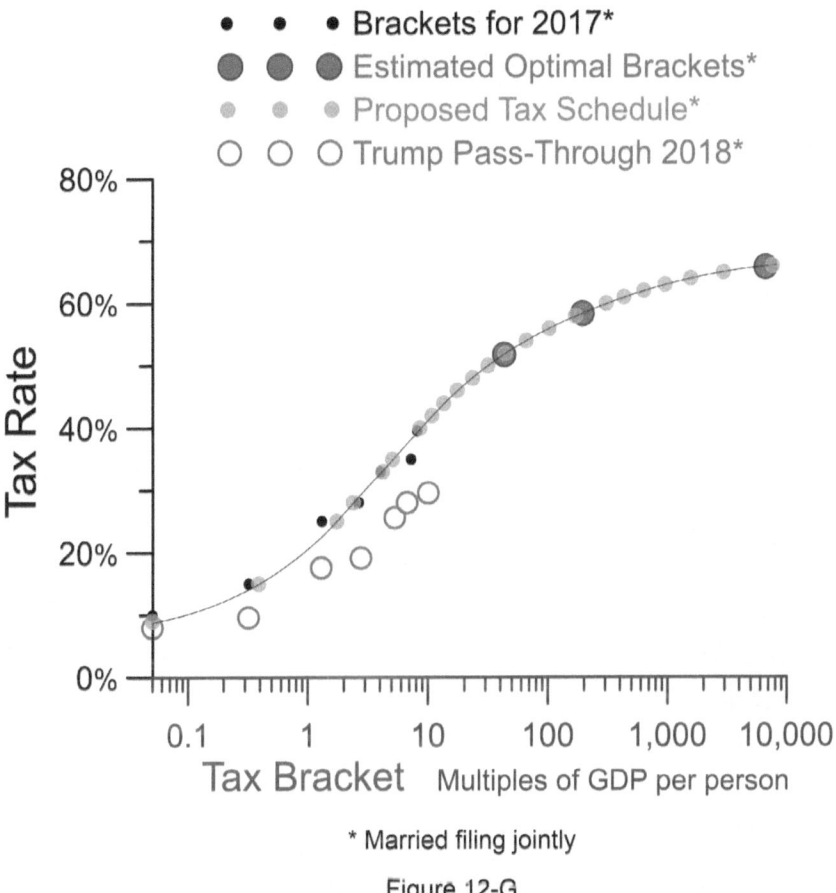

* Married filing jointly

Figure 12-G

This pattern could easily connect with the black dots which are the more permanent tax rates or with the gray circles which show Trump's seven brackets scheduled to be in place eight years. Both Trump's brackets and those prior to Trump have a bit of a zigzag pattern rather than a smooth trajectory. (A small housekeeping note: the bottom bracket of 10 percent starts at zero dollars of taxable income, but a logarithmic scale does not go to zero, so I plot it at 0.05 multiples of GDP/p.)

After calculating the three optimal points I created a smooth trajectory that runs through those points and roughly through the existing permanent tax brackets.

The proposal shows twenty-three brackets as small gray dots in Figure 12-G. You may remember the charts on the number of brackets and growth from Chapter 3, where each additional 15.5 brackets corresponded to raising the growth rate a full percent. It might be more pro-growth to have thirty or even fifty brackets on the trajectory, but using twenty-three makes a good example tax schedule.

The sixteen additional brackets by themselves should raise our growth rate from 2.1 to 3.1 percent . . . but it gets much better. This plan restores the incentive for our very elite to grow their businesses that has been missing since 1942.

In Figure 12-G the gray circles show the Trump brackets discounted 20 percent for the pass-through tax rate that may influence how much revenue gets drawn out of businesses as personal income.

The pass-through marginal tax rate at the top bracket of $600,000, roughly 10 GDP/p is 29.6 percent. The growth optimizing marginal tax rate for 10 GDP/p is likely 40 percent. While it is not clear how many businesses will get the full pass-through discount, the 37 percent top rate is still below the optimal. For personal incomes that rise up into the millions or hundreds of millions the 29.6 percent or 37 percent marginal rate falls dramatically below the growth optimizing level.

This 29.6 percent rate is barely half the 50 percent top rate that led to the strongest year of growth in the last sixty-five years. In the proposal the 50 percent rate comes with a bracket of 31.5 GDP/p, about $1.9 million in 2018 which should be high enough to prevent the junk investments that came with this tax rate in the 1980s.

The proposed schedule starts at 9 percent, rather than 10 percent. In 2017 the proposed schedule would have saved $418 of tax on $50,000 of taxable income and $2,828 of tax on income of $100,000.

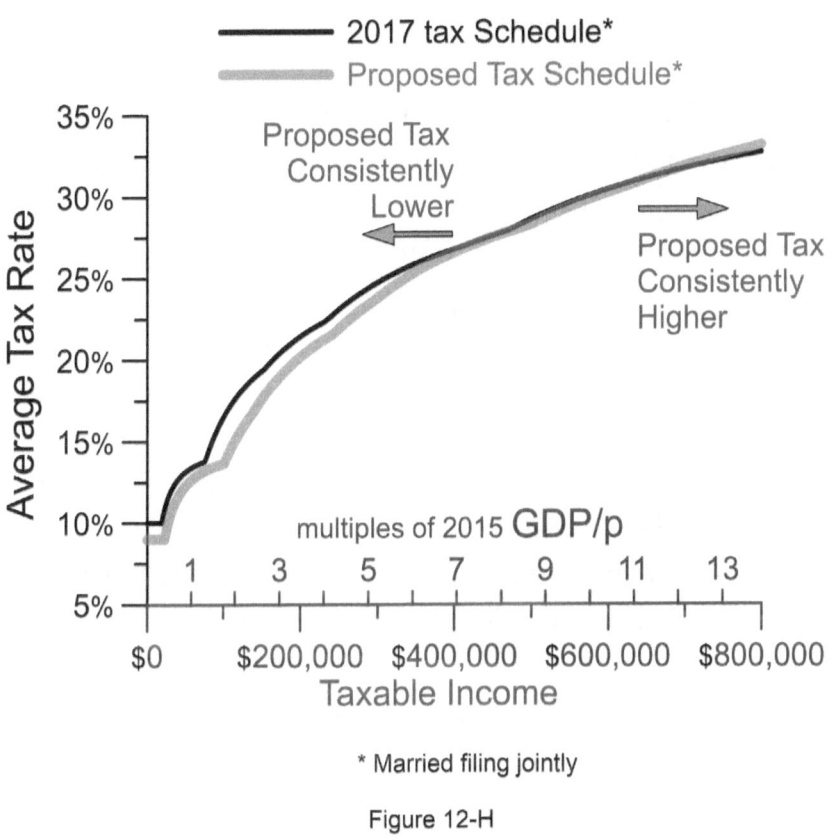

Figure 12-H

Tax-cuts for the 97%

The black line in Figure 12-H shows the average tax rate for a given amount of ordinary income in 2017. The gray line shows the average with the proposed brackets in Figure 12-G. When the Trump tax cut for personal income expires in a few years, the gaps will be larger than shown in Figure 12-H since adjusting brackets for inflation will be less tax friendly than adjusting for GDP per person.

This tax plan is a win-win-*win* for the economy compared to the 2017 tax rates. The incentive to work improves because the average tax rate on almost all wage-earners goes down, and the marginal rate drops for most of them as well; the average tax rate on business owners taking less than $400,000 of income will be noticeably lower as well, which improves the incentive to run a business; the marginal tax rate on the people with the most potential to grow the economy is significantly higher, thereby creating more incentive to avoid tax by growing businesses.

At $665,000 of ordinary taxable income, the average rate for both the 2017 brackets and the proposed brackets is 31.36 percent—so there is equal incentive to run a business; but the proposed marginal rate would have been 42 percent in 2017, while the actual 2017 rate was 39.6 percent. So with the same incentive to run the business, the proposed brackets give stronger incentive to put money in the big pocket and grow the business.

Compared to the temporary Trump tax cuts the proposal would only lower taxes for people with taxable income below about $33,000 and for income between about $96,000 and $122,000. This is where the gray line is lower than the black line in Figure 12-H1

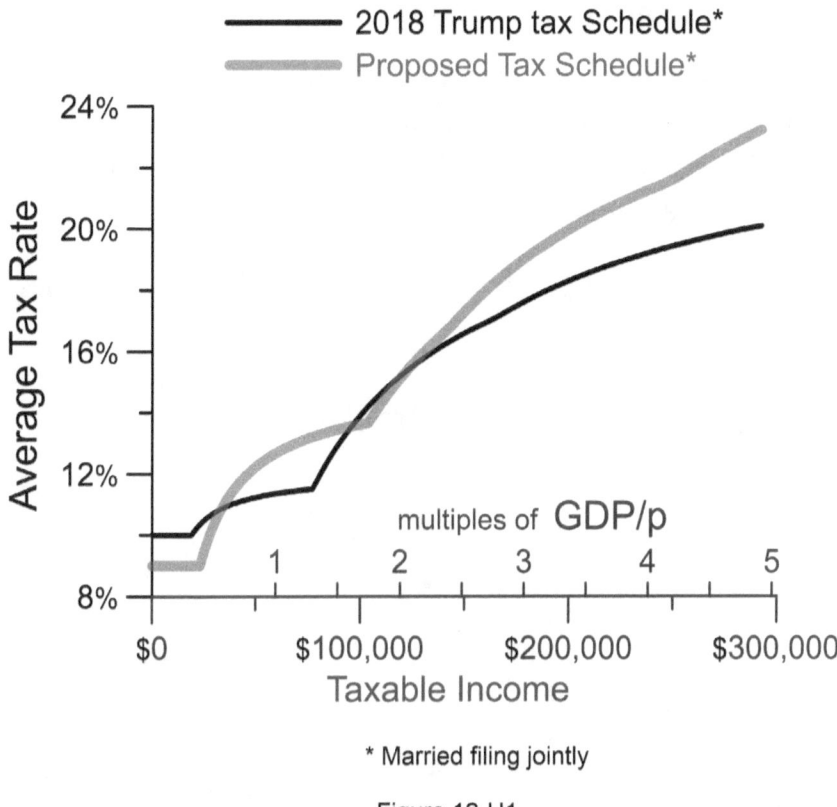

* Married filing jointly

Figure 12-H1

While the Trump tax plan greatly reduces the big pocket incentive to avoid taxes by growing businesses, a small portion of that negative growth influence should be offset with a bigger small pocket incentive to work and run businesses.

Most of my analysis deals with the big pocket incentive which appears to dominate the long term growth rate. If the small pocket incentive could be shown to have a meaningful impact on growth it would make sense to change the 15 percent tax rate in the proposal to the 12 percent rate that Trump uses. This would make the proposed average tax rate lower than Trump's plan up through about $177,000.

Deeper Look into Capital Gains

We can now work through a similar exercise for the capital-gains tax rate and the residual growth from the top marginal rate. In the 1 to 57 GDP/p shown in Figure 12-I, the growth-optimizing tax rate appears to be 28 percent.

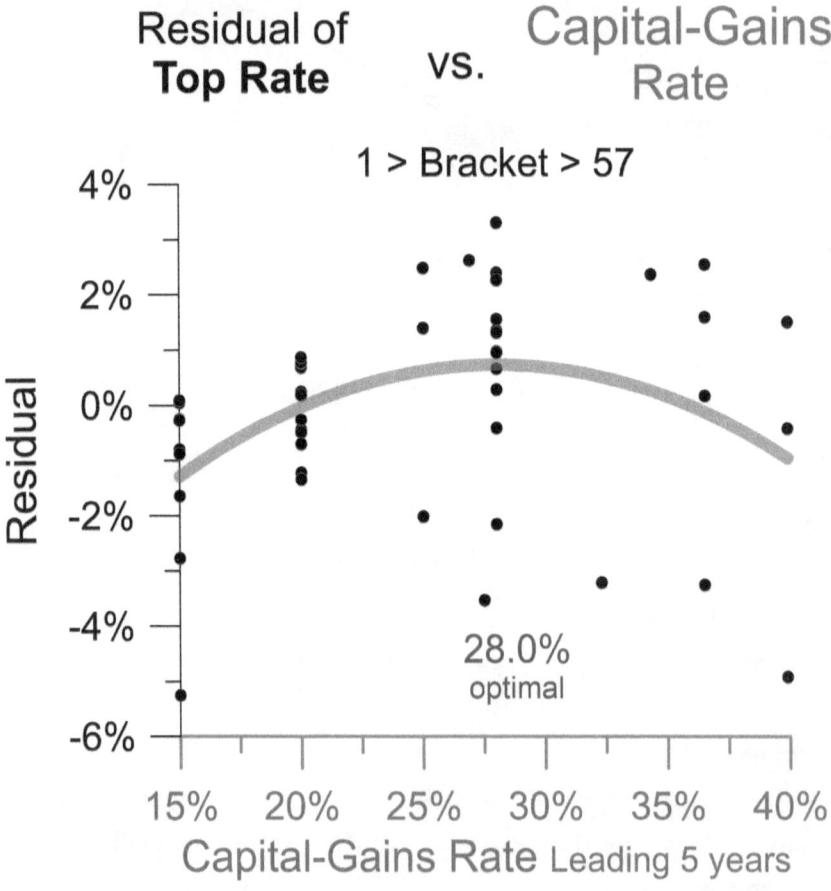

Figure 12-I

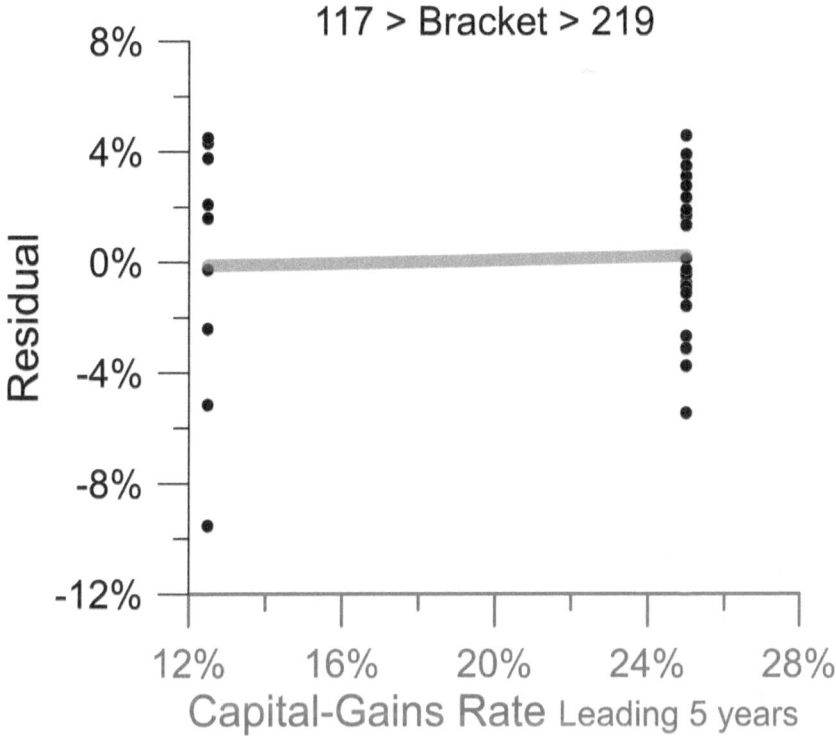

Figure 12-J

With brackets from 117 to 219 GDP/p, the years influenced by the 25 percent capital-gains rate had a slightly higher average residual-growth rate than the ones influenced by the 12.5 percent capital-gains tax rate. The reasonable conclusion would be that the tax rate should be at least 25 percent. Conclusions beyond that take some interpretation and assumptions. (I am already assuming the middle-bracket data in Figure 12-J should not have a lower tax rate than the low-bracket data in Figure 12-I.)

For brackets above 649 GDP/p, the best-fit curvilinear line suggests a 47.3 percent capital-gains rate brings the best growth.

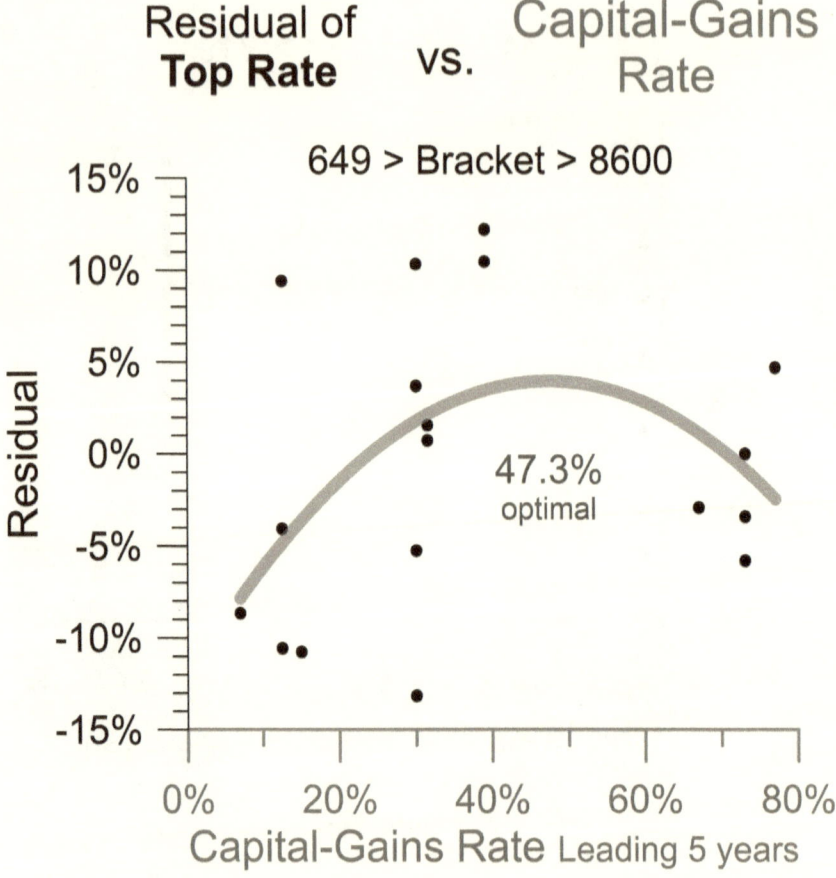

Figure 12-K

I tried including the data points from the middle bracket with both the low-bracket data and the high-bracket data. This weakened the fit with the low-bracket data; while it fit reasonably with the high-bracket data, I think the high-bracket data stands better by itself, so I am not making an optimal data point for the middle-bracket data. I only plotted two optimal points in Figure 12-L to help estimate the growth-maximizing path for capital-gains tax rates.

I will use the 43 GDP/p and 6,600 GDP/p that I used for the top marginal rates.

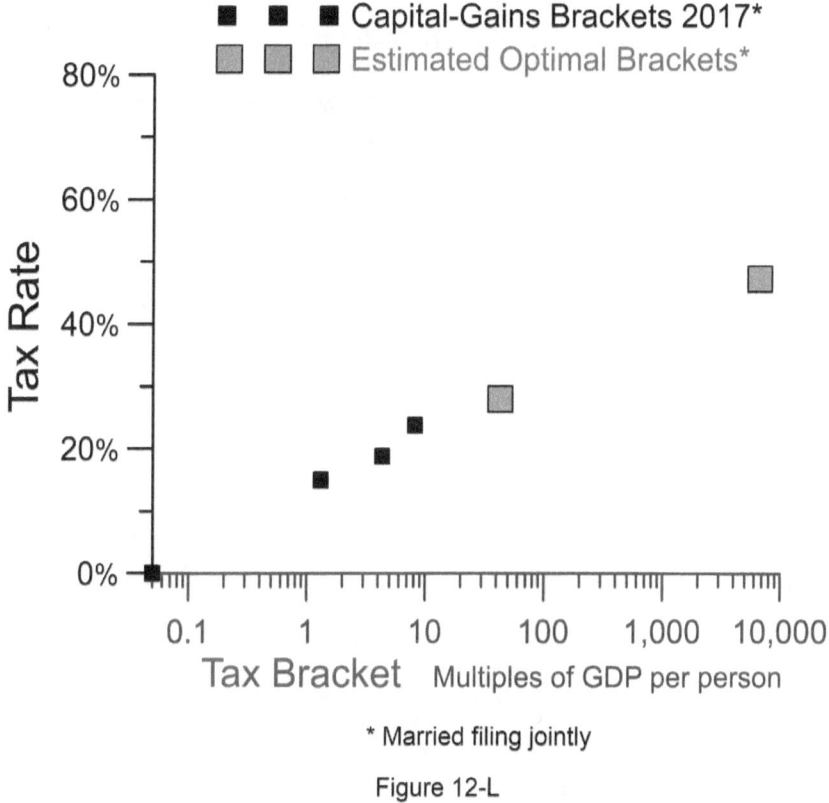

*Married filing jointly

Figure 12-L

The two optimal points, along with the existing capital-gains brackets, would appear to be on a logarithmic path (which will appear linear, since the *x*-axis for the tax bracket is on a log scale).

The proposed brackets in Figure 12-M follow the current pattern, where there is no tax on long-term capital gain for people with an average income. I am not sure how to analyze if that helps growth or not, so I left it in tact and actually increased the amount that could be tax-free.

I left a big gap from the 28 percent bracket that begins at 44 GDP/p to the next bracket at 630 GDP/p, since the middle-bracket data did not suggest that the rate should be higher than the 28 percent estimated for the low-bracket data. Also, since labor and trade were sensitive to a capital-gains rate that was too high, I wanted to be sure a marginal tax rate above 28 percent on capital gains only comes into play at a very high bracket.

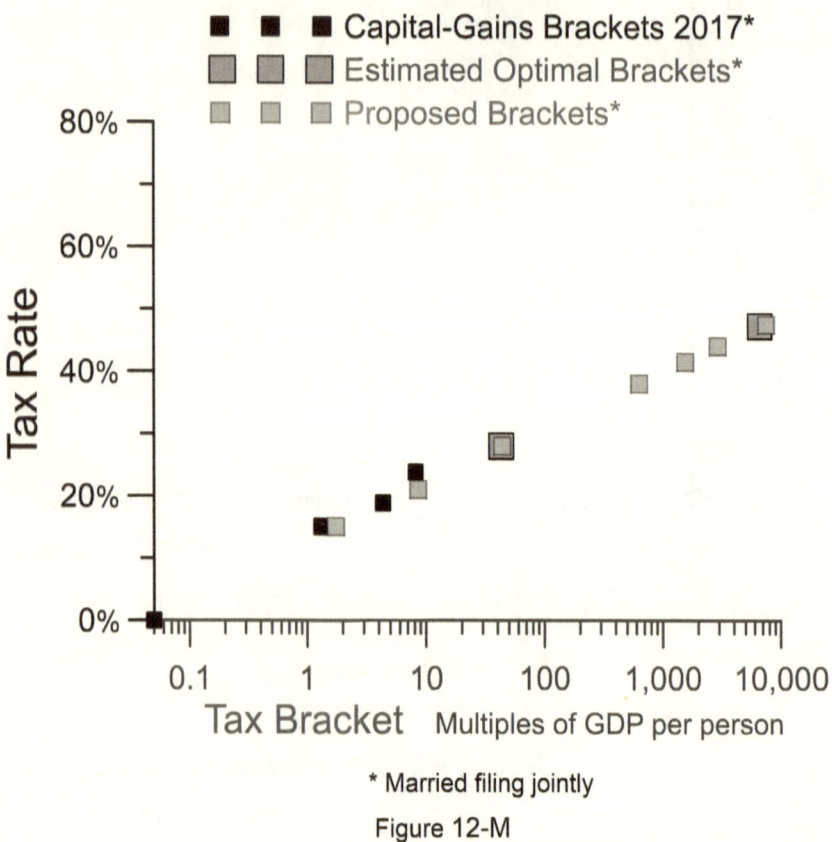

* Married filing jointly

Figure 12-M

Best Tax Schedule Ever

Figures 12-N and 12-O show the proposed tax brackets in graph- and table-form (respectively). This tax schedule accommodates the concepts in this book, but might not take into account all the considerations that would need to go into a tax schedule that was actually adopted. It is also worth mentioning that I only made a schedule for "married filing jointly," since that schedule has been the basis of my research.

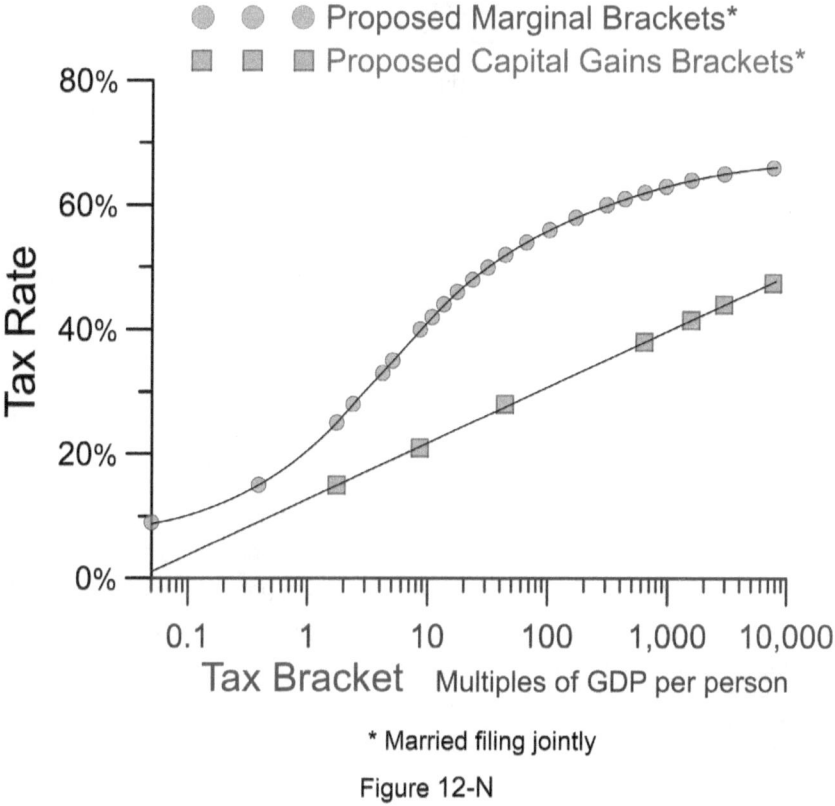

* Married filing jointly

Figure 12-N

Proposed Tax Rates and Brackets*

Tax Rates:		Income Brackets in Multiples of GDP per person:		GDP/p converted to Dollars	
Ordinary Income	Capital-Gains Income	Above	and Below	2017	2018
9%	0%	0	0.39	$0	$0
15%	"	0.39	1.75	$22,500	$23,200
25%	15%	1.75	2.4	$101,000	$104,100
28%	"	2.4	4.2	$138,000	$143,000
33%	"	4.2	5.1	$242,000	$250,000
35%	"	5.1	8.6	$294,000	$303,000
40%	21%	8.6	10.8	$495,000	$511,000
42%	"	10.8	13.5	$622,000	$642,000
44%	"	13.5	17.5	$777,000	$803,000
46%	"	17.5	23.5	$1,010,000	$1,041,000
48%	"	23.5	31.5	$1,350,000	$1,400,000
50%	"	31.5	44	$1,810,000	$1,870,000
52%	28%	44	66	$2,530,000	$2,620,000
54%	"	66	103	$3,800,000	$3,930,000
56%	"	103	170	$5,930,000	$6,130,000
58%	"	170	305	$9,790,000	$10,110,000
60%	"	305	430	$17,600,000	$18,100,000
61%	"	430	630	$24,800,000	$25,600,000
62%	38%	630	950	$36,300,000	$37,500,000
63%	"	950	1,550	$54,700,000	$56,500,000
64%	41.5%	1,550	2,900	$89,300,000	$92,200,000
65%	44%	2,900	7,500	$167,000,000	$172,000,000
66%	47.5%	7,500		$432,000,000	$446,000,000

*Married filing jointly

Figure 12-O

Topping the Best Growth Ever?

If we use the growth model from Chapter 3 and plug in the 66 percent top rate, the 47.5 percent capital-gains rate, and the 7,500-GDP/p top bracket, it suggests the growth rate would rise to 7.2 percent after the two-year lag for the top rate; to 9.5 percent after the three-year lag for the top bracket; and to 11.7 percent after the lag for the capital-gains rate.

You, like me, should be skeptical of those high estimates.

The period of 1934 to 1943 was the strongest ten-year period of growth in U.S. history, annualizing 10.3 percent. The model's high estimates are fitted around that growth. The context of that period is vastly different from today, of course, so, unfortunately, we probably can't expect to recreate that growth now. However, one of those important differences is completely within our control.

The strongest ten-year growth in U.S. history began when a ten-year time horizon was hardwired into the tax code. Starting in 1934, the holding period to get the full long-term capital-gains discount was set to—you guessed it—ten years. There were partial discounts with shorter holding periods, but for ultra-high-income people, minimizing taxes required a ten-year outlook.

While there are a few visionaries who would create great businesses and industries as a lifetime endeavor regardless of the tax code, a long-term tax incentive should encourage more long-term behavior and help align the interests of elites with the general welfare of the country.

We should recreate that ten-year holding period. So, if assets are held for ten years, you would get the full discount (shown in the above tax schedules). I would propose partial discounts for holding assets for one year, two years, and five years, where you get 10 percent of the discount, 20 percent, and 50 percent (respectively).

Let's consider the effect of the proposed tax code on our most elite business owners. Practically everyone dislikes paying taxes, right? Logic follows, then, that if you're paying hundreds of thousands of dollars in taxes, the dislike intensifies. Now if you were paying a few hundred *million*, wouldn't you be trying to figure out how to pay less tax?

In the tax schedule above, the marginal tax bite hits 52 percent around the $2.6-million mark and 58 percent around $10 million. At this level of income, you would be paying millions in taxes and the big tax-free pocket becomes mighty attractive. Avoiding the tax means building a business or a portfolio of businesses as a lifetime endeavor, or at least focusing on a ten-year time horizon to get the lower capital-gains tax rate.

As big as the impact is on elites who own a portfolio of businesses, the bigger growth impact may come from changing CEO behavior in those major corporations. The average tenure of a CEO is about six years. This time period gives them one shot at a pay-bonanza worth several lifetimes of income. The combination of the business cycle, incentive pay, and historically low marginal tax rates creates a huge opportunity.

The incentive pay often comes in the form of stock options, which must be held for a minimum of three to five years. If CEOs can string three to five years of stellar earnings-growth together, they can often hit the pay-bonanza.

If performance is measured over less than six years, CEOs can play a game of "heads I win, tails you lose" with their compensation. They can take big risks that pay off handsomely while the economy expands, while employees and shareholders are left holding the bag if the economy goes into recession.

If you don't care much about the long-term, there are easy ways to drive up short-term profits. A CEO could defer maintenance on equipment; he could avoid investments that have a payoff more than a few years out; he could cut the workforce; he could leverage the corporation with debt; he could use the debt to buy back company stock. This often happens near a stock-market peak, as CEOs try to squeeze more out of their performance pay.

If the time horizon to maximize after-tax pay is more than ten years, the above strategies likely backfire. As Warren Buffet says, "You don't know who's swimming naked until the tide goes out." And sure enough, so far a recession has come or the tide has gone out at least once every ten years.

Deferring maintenance usually costs more in the long run. Investments that solidify a company's future, on the other hand, often have a payout longer than ten years. Cutting the workforce harms morale and often hurts growth in the long run. To pull off major advances, a corporation needs inspired, dedicated workers. Leveraging with debt means profits fall faster in the next downturn, which increases the risk of bankruptcy.

If you can't cash in your performance pay from your last year as CEO until ten years after you're gone, you will take great care to ensure talented, ethical people are in the leadership pipeline.

Trump's tax plan took a small step in the right direction: hedge fund managers organized as a standard or "C" corporation will have to hold assets for three years to get their compensation known as a "carried interest" taxed at the lower capital gains tax rate. This may also apply to hedge fund managers organized as a pass-through entity, but it may take a court case to be sure.

A ten-year time horizon more closely matches the interest of a hedge fund manager and more importantly a CEO with the long-term well-being of stockholders, employees, and consumers. It could help push growth above 5 percent, but probably wouldn't get us the 11.7 percent mentioned above. That period that grew from the

Put Money in Your Pocket | 167

bottom of the Great Depression and included rapid growth during WWII will likely not be matched.

Using the model data from the last forty-eight years (the low-bracket data), and just implementing the tax brackets through a 52 percent marginal rate and a 28 percent capital-gains rate, suggests growth would raise to 4.1 percent in 2020 and 4.4 percent in 2023. With this faster growth, the middle class would soon be paying more taxes than they are now—even though their rate would be lower.

In six years, when the tax increases start raising the share of the pie going to labor, they will pay a good bit more tax—but their higher after-tax income will make it all worthwhile. On the other hand, the wealthy will be paying less tax—because they will take much less taxable income—as they grow the value of their businesses at a much faster rate. The faster growth of their wealth within their businesses will more than make up for their smaller short-term incomes.

Implementing the full plan above should raise growth above the 4.4 percent rate—and perhaps substantially so. However, it might be prudent to implement the plan in steps. Raising the top rate and capital-gains rate to 52 percent and 28 percent (respectively) could be an appropriate first step to returning to actual pro-growth tax policy. We could add these brackets, watch the results for about six years, and when they prove themselves we could add more of the higher brackets.

If we optimize the tax bracket for a given marginal tax rate, keeping that optimal bracket requires adjusting by GDP/p. Adjusting for inflation is better than no adjustment, of course, but it doesn't fully do the job. GDP/p has grown 5.4 percent-a-year over the last fifty years, and CPI is at only 4.1 percent. Over this period, adjusting for GDP/p would have raised brackets close to twice what adjusting for inflation actually did.

If we adjust brackets by GDP/p, the wealthy can give themselves tax-cuts by growing the economy—and the faster GDP/p grows, the bigger the increase in every bracket. More income gets taxed at lower marginal rates. Seven brackets would amount to seven tax-cuts for the wealthy; with twenty-three brackets, it would be twenty-three tax-cuts.

When they cut taxes for themselves, taxes are cut for everyone.

We would all have incentive to bake a bigger pie together.

Use Genius Wisely

Above I mentioned there were three additional points to making growth stronger. The first one—the biggest of the three—was creating the ten-year time horizon with the tax code; the second one involves redirecting genius to benefit society and the third and final one tweaks the little-pocket, big-pocket decision.

Some of the brightest people around are busy writing black-box trading algorithms to generate huge incomes from how stock prices wiggle over a nanosecond or a minute or a day or a month. For all the good this does society, it's kind of like taking some of the most promising graduates from the best schools and paying them big bucks to watch their bellybuttons.

The financial industry operates a bit like a pipeline, taking individuals' savings and investments and delivering them to the companies and industries that are creating our future wellbeing.

We are all better off when the people operating this pipeline do a good job of allocating capital to the businesses that are best able to satisfy the needs and wants of the people. We want the people who are good at this to end up with huge after-tax income over the course of their lives. This is how the financial system should help the long-term real economy work.

Unfortunately, the short-term financial economy has drilled lots of little holes in the pipeline with a wealth-sucker at each hole, reducing the reward at the end of the pipeline for the workers and entrepreneurs who are actually creating the wealth. Plugging these holes helps make long-term real behavior more profitable than short-term financial behavior—especially for our geniuses.

At the beginning of that record ten-year period of growth mentioned earlier (1934-44) the Securities and Exchange Act of 1934 plugged lots of the holes wealth-suckers had bored into the pipeline. Many, especially the "wealth-suckers," complained of burdensome regulations and warned the nation was going socialistic. In retrospect, it is hard to argue with the 10.3 percent growth rate that followed.

Many of today's holes in the pipeline involve short-term trading that has nothing to do with allocating real capital to meet the needs of mankind. One proposal I've heard to reduce short-term trading is a small tax on financial transactions. The tax would be barely high enough to make frequent transactions less profitable. A likely valid criticism of such a tax is it would drive transactions to markets that did not have such a tax.

It might be more effective to surtax investment positions held for a very short time—sort of a reverse of the long-term capital-gains discount. Perhaps a gain on a position held for less than forty-eight hours would be taxed at 90 percent; a position held between two and thirty days at 80 percent; between thirty and sixty days at 70 percent; and if the position were held between sixty days and a year, it would be taxed as ordinary income (as it is now).

Of course, after a year, the capital-gains discount would start kicking in. We don't want the taxes on short-term trading to raise much tax revenue; instead, our goal is to make long-term "real" behavior more profitable than short-term financial behavior. As with the capital-gains discount, the surtax would not apply to one's primary business; for example, a retailer would not owe surtax on the difference between retail and wholesale prices.

All the wealth-suckers in the financial industry would hate this, but if the number of shares traded in a day dropped from a billion to a hundred million, would it reduce the production of any good or service that actually benefits people? Not likely, in fact, greatly reducing short-term trading could free up a great amount of time, effort, resources, and focus for more beneficial endeavors. The transaction cost of a single trade or investment would go up, but the total cost of trading would plummet and improved long-term investments would increase our well-being. Does anything that will matter ten or a hundred years from now really fluctuate in a forty-eight-hour period?

Maybe the reason we don't have flying cars yet is that our rocket scientists have been too busy trading stocks to invent them.

Protecting the Big Pocket

The third tweak to tax policy would change how dividends are taxed. Starting in 2003, dividends have been taxed at the rate of long-term capital gains, which increases the attractiveness of moving money from the big pocket to the little pocket through dividends. Growth since 2003 has been lousy, but I don't know how to discern what part, if any, of the weakness is due to dividend taxation. From 1913 to 2002, dividends were taxed as ordinary income.

This 2003 change was made based on the accounting argument that stockholders are double-taxed: once by the corporate income tax and then by personal taxes on dividends.

We noted in Chapter 3 that the burden of paying the corporate income tax may be passed on to workers in lower wages and consumers in higher prices. Keep in mind, the real economy is the production, distribution, and consumption of goods and services. Money and accounting are one step removed from this reality—kind of like a map is a level of abstraction removed from the actual territory.

A company's after-tax profit likely stems from the level of competition the company faces in the marketplace. The double-taxation claim of accounting likely hides the economic reality. If workers and consumers are bearing the burden of the corporate income tax, taxing dividends at a lower rate may be a tax-cut for the wealthy that encourages pulling money out of the big pocket into the small pocket and exacerbates all the economic problems we've noted in Chapters 3 through 8.

Since no one is really sure how the burden of the corporate income tax divides out, I think it would be reasonable in the above tax plan to tax dividends at the rate of capital gains held for one year, but not the full discount for a ten-year holding period.

Tax Estates?

Another controversy is how to tax estates. For many years I thought the estate tax was helping keep America a meritocracy, where your position in life was determined more by your effort than by what family you were born into, and that it would help keep our nation a democracy rather than become a plutocracy. While this could be the correct view, I realized in writing this book that I don't have quantitative data to back it up.

If we don't have an estate tax, the income tax plan above becomes even more important to prosperity. We need those receiving multi-billion-dollar inheritances to have incentive to build wealth in the big pocket, rather than become a net drain on society by consuming more than they produce. The proposed tax plan would help fulfill the idea in Luke 12:48, "To whom much is given, much shall be required."

In this chapter we tried to use all the data we have to estimate the growth-optimizing combinations of marginal tax rates and brackets for both ordinary and capital-gains income. We created a tax schedule using optimal estimates. We recommended adjusting tax brackets by GDP\p rather than inflation.

The proposed tax schedule would give more small-pocket incentive than the existing permanent tax brackets and could be adjusted to maintain the small pocket incentive afforded by the temporary Trump tax brackets. The proposed tax schedule dramatically increases the big pocket incentive to grow businesses, especially above the current top bracket of $600,000. We looked at the benefits of creating a long-term ten-year incentive in the tax code using capital gains. We considered a couple of ways to encourage more productive effort and to plug some of the holes in the wealth pipeline that reward the actual wealth-creators.

We suggested implementing the plan in phases and only going to the next phase after the previous one has proved itself. Historical correlation suggests the initial phase of the plan would raise the average GDP growth rate to at least 4.4 percent. We also saw how this plan becomes even more vital if there is no estate tax.

In the next chapter, we show what voters have to do if we want a chance at restoring long-term prosperity.

Chapter 13
Training Politicians

We have met the enemy and he is us. —Walt Kelly, Pogo

In this chapter we will show how we trained our politicians to give us weak growth, including the great recession and financial crisis. We will go through elections where we punished politicians who moved marginal tax rates closer to the growth-optimizing levels and rewarded the ones who took us farther down the wrong path. Restoring prosperity will be a simple matter of training our politicians in the opposite manner by voting differently.

When I was in the sixth grade, *Pogo* became one of my favorite comic strips (it didn't make much sense to me before then). For weeks, frenzy built among the forest animals about some outside enemy that would destroy and trash their forest; it culminated in a rally or protest, complete with signs, banners, enthusiasm, and speeches. After the rally, Pogo observed all the trash left on the forest floor and said, "We have met the enemy and he is us." I remember thinking fear itself was the enemy that led to trashing their own forest.

If we can be made fearful, we are much easier to manipulate. Republicans have been trained to fear and blame Democrats for the woes of the land and, of course, Democrats have the same training regarding Republicans. We blame Washington and money in politics, the media, and on and on.

We are powerless to fix our economic problems until we recognize that we as citizens and voters brought the problems upon ourselves.

We Voted for Crisis

The next two figures show tax changes and how growth responded. The first one focuses on the change in tax rates; the second on the resulting growth. We will see how votes in reaction to tax changes brought the weak growth, deficits, and stagnant wages we complain about and fear.

The shaded blocks (*A–F*) in Figure 13-A show several tax-rate changes. Each block marks the change to either the top rate or the capital gains, and the corresponding change to the combined rate shown by the light-gray line overlaying the plot of GDP. Each tax-rate axis is scaled to show the influence on growth. So a move in one of the tax rates has an identical move in the combined tax rate, which is a model of the two tax rates.

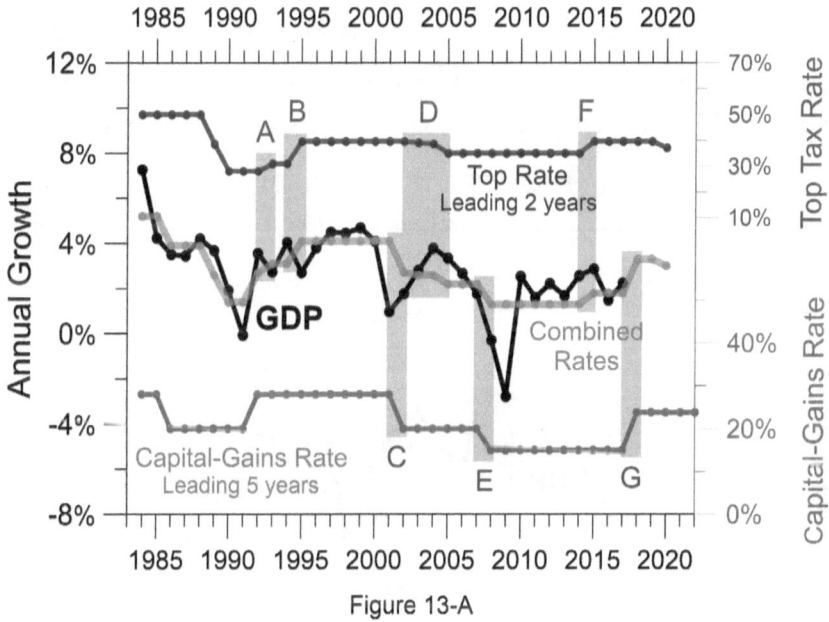

Figure 13-A

The path to weakness began quite innocently. President Reagan cutting the top rate to 50 percent from the too-high 70 percent helped improve growth. The robust economy in 1984 led to the widest Electoral College victory since 1936. This was the last tax-cut to result in stronger growth. It paved the political path of destructive tax-cuts as a winning political strategy—and raising taxes a path to political death.

In 1991 George H. W. Bush raised the top rate (*A* on the chart); in 1992 we voted him out of office. In 1993 a Democratic Congress raised the top rate (*B*); in 1994 we voted them out of office.

"Put tax-cutters in charge!" we screamed with our votes.

The capital-gains rate was cut in 1997 (*C*). We elected more tax-cutters. The 2001 tax-cut lowered the marginal rate in 2001 and 2002 (*D*). The 2003 cut lowered the top rate (*D*) and the capital-gains rate (*E*). Then we increased the majority of Republican tax-cutters in the 2004 election.

In 2013 Democrats let several of the Bush tax-cuts expire (*F* and *G*). The Medicare surtax on capital gains—part of Obamacare—also took effect in 2013 (*G*). In 2014 we voted to give the tax-raising Democrats the smallest percentage control of Congress since 1930.

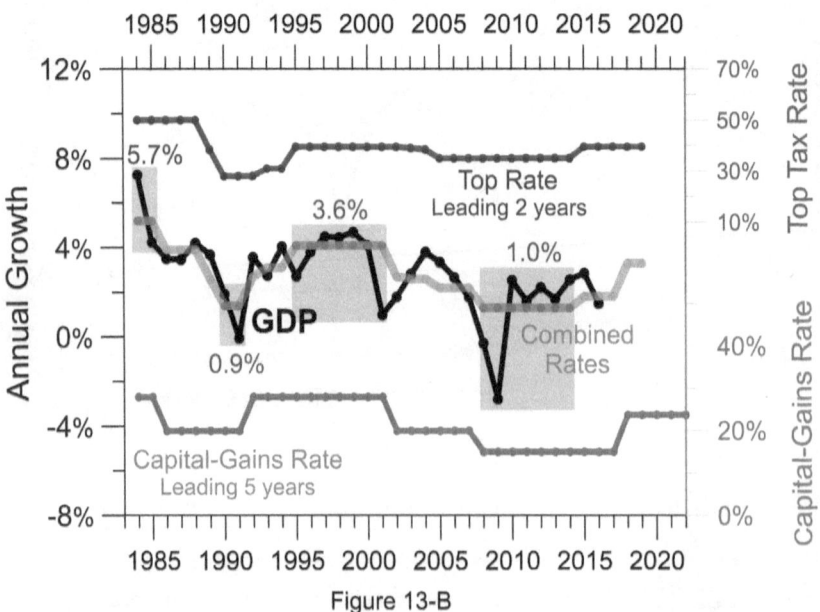

Figure 13-B

Our misinformed good intentions replaced politicians who moved marginal tax rates closer to the growth-optimizing level with ones who moved tax rates further *below* the growth-optimizing level. We got a combination of a 35 percent top tax rate with a 15 percent capital-gains rate for ten years.

Using the respective lead times of two and five years, their influences overlapped seven years. Those seven years annualized growing 1 percent (as you can see in the shaded box farthest to the right in Figure 13-B).

We trained our politicians to give us 1 percent growth.

When the economy's underlying growth rate is 3.5 percent, it typically grows between 4 and 5 percent during an expansion and then shrinks a percentage or two during the contraction. With an underlying growth rate of 1 percent from 2008 through 2014, the economy shrank 3.9 percent during the contraction, then only grew at 2.1 percent during the expansion.

We didn't mean to . . . but we *voted* for the financial crisis and great recession.

Now before I start suggesting how you vote, let's drive the point home. Take another look at Figure 13-B. The two years influenced by Reagan's top rate of 50 percent and Carter's capital-gains rate of 28 percent grew at 5.7 percent. The best growth in this period came with the highest marginal rates.

The two years influenced by the 28 percent top rate and 20 percent capital-gains rate only annualized 0.9 percent. Bill Clinton's 39.6 percent top rate and Reagan returning the capital-gains rate to 28 percent corresponded with a 3.6 percent growth rate. This strong growth rate even includes the 2001 recession.

The chart is like clockwork: when marginal rates were high, growth was strong; when tax rates went down, growth faltered; when rates went up, growth improved; when taxes were cut, growth weakened. The chart also implies growth will strengthen in 2018.

Briefly, let's recognize our votes were responsible for the shrinking middle class, stagnant real wages, America's declining place in the world, slow growth, selling trillions of dollars of U.S. assets to foreign nations, the largest budget deficits ever, increasing the national debt 250 percent, inflating and popping asset bubbles, and our financial insecurity.

OK, time to move on. Let's collectively forgive ourselves and everyone else. At some point, almost everyone believed low marginal tax rates were a good idea. They seemed like a good idea at the time, right? If you start to feel guilty or like blaming someone else, remember we all did the best we knew how.

However, now that we know better it is time to *vote* better.

Stop Punishing the Good

The good news? This experience shows we the people have the power to train our politicians. Training them is easy. All it takes is for a few politicians to lose their place in office for doing the wrong thing, and a majority of the rest will fall into line.

We should not expect our politicians to do the right thing if we punish them for it. While our Founding Fathers risked their lives and all they possessed to create this nation, the common tendency of mankind remains a bit more self-serving.

If we are serious about prosperity we must vote against any politician who continues advocating a top marginal rate, a top bracket, or a capital-gains rate that is far below the growth optimizing level. We must also vote against anyone proposing to add high marginal tax rates without having high-enough brackets to keep average tax rates low.

This includes voting against any U.S. Representative or Senator who proposes a flat tax or replacing the income tax with a sales tax. Both plans would have lower marginal rates than what brought on the Great Depression. The latter would in effect have a zero percent marginal income tax rate.

If you continue to vote politicians into national office who refuse to raise marginal tax rates closer to their growth-optimizing levels or propose cutting them even further, it is as if you are voting for your neighbor to lose their job in the next recession. You encourage elites to pull more revenue away from production within a business to enable lavish consumption, suck in imports, drive asset prices into bubbles, and spend more on politics.

It's like saying, *I don't care if the workers' share of GDP continues declining. I enjoy stories like, "Last week so-and-so got laid off. Now I'm doing her job and my job, but I'm not getting paid any more. The stress is making things harder at home too."*

If we are going to fix this, it's important we learn the right lesson. In the Great Depression we didn't learn the lesson because voters blamed Republicans rather than bad tax policy.

Republicans went from twelve years in the Whitehouse and 65 percent control of Congress to twenty years of Democrats in the Whitehouse and Democrats briefly holding 81 percent of Congress. If Republicans had stronger numbers, FDR probably would not have been able to make that horrible mistake of dropping the top bracket 96 percent while raising the top rate to 94 percent.

If Republicans had learned the lesson, they wouldn't have put into place the bad tax policy that contributed to the great recession and weak growth the last thirteen years. If Democrats had learned the lesson, they wouldn't say "We want to make the rich pay more tax," but rather "Let's get rates and brackets that encourage the wealthy to grow businesses and make the nation prosper."

Knowing the history of how tax rates correlate with growth made the 2016 election quite ironic. Hillary Clinton and Bernie Sanders proposed marginal tax rates that were pro-growth and would have encouraged growing the big pocket, but instead of talking about growth focused on making the rich pay more.

Donald Trump, along with all the Republican candidates, proposed anti-growth, pour-money-into-the-small-pocket policies, and claimed they would make the economy grow faster. Trump now has his tax cut and after the two year lag we must watch what happens to growth in 2020 and beyond.

We don't want the rich to pay more. We want them to build the economy more. It's up to us to vote for them to do it. If we want people like George Soros and the Koch brothers to spend less money on politics and more money growing the economy, we must vote to give them higher marginal tax rates.

In this chapter we saw how our votes trained our politicians to give us weak growth, and how all the problems described in this book go along with pulling lots of revenue out of businesses and into the small pocket.

We saw how we punished the people who were giving us pro-growth policies and empowered the wolf wearing a sheepskin. While it's appropriate to forgive people, including politicians and the wolves who were on the wrong side of tax policy in the past, we probably cannot fix this problem until we kick out some incumbents who stay on the wrong side.

It is time to vote for prosperity. It would be wonderful to vote for higher brackets and marginal tax rates in 2018 and 2020. However, as we'll see in the next chapter, the 2024 election may be our best bet to put the country on the path to sustained widespread prosperity.

Chapter 14
Looking Ahead

In this chapter, I will suggest how you should decide who understands the economy well enough for you to follow. We'll look at implications of President Trump's tax cut (based on models from previous chapters). We'll see how the lagged effect of the capital-gains rate could make Trump look good going into the 2020 election, but his tax-cuts should harm economic growth by 2024.

The best test of understanding includes being able to predict what reality will be. Einstein's theory of relativity includes gravity bending light. When his prediction of how much the sun would bend the course of light from stars on the other side was verified during a solar eclipse in 1919, it cemented his reputation as a scientific genius.

Following the great recession and financial crisis, it was a bit humorous listening to explanations of its cause from people who did not see it coming. Almost all the so-called causes were merely extensions of preconceived notions about how the world works, often with a political agenda behind them.

While the last twelve years of data reinforce my conclusions made in 2006, you may, perhaps even appropriately, view all the correlations in this book as a curious coincidence. This book's litmus test will be if the forecasts below turn out reasonably accurate.

Below we attempt to plug President Trump's tax policy on personal income into models of growth, employee compensation, and trade in order to estimate what will happen out to 2025.

The pass-through discount complicates the attempt. I expect the pass-through tax rate rather than the top rate of 37 percent will be a better measure of the marginal tax rate elite business owners face when deciding whether to pull more revenue out of businesses as personal income or avoid taxes by using more of the revenue to grow the business. However, not all revenue business owners pull out as personal income will qualify for the pass through rate. Not all the businesses that qualify for the pass-through rate will get the full 20 percent discount. To get the full 20 percent discount that in effect lowers the top rate from 37 to 29.6 percent a business must have a sufficient combination of capital and payroll expense. The rules governing this discount are not settled and may not be fully settled until courts review some of the attempts to get that discount.

The marginal rate elite business owners face in the decision of how much revenue to pull out as income will be between 29.6 and 37 percent. I am taking a stab in the dark and guessing the average effect will be as though the top rate was 34 percent.

	Through 2017	Trump Pass-Through
Top Tax Rate	39.6%	29.6%·····34%·····37%
Capital Gains Rate	23.8%	23.8%
Top Bracket in GDP/p	8.2	10.1

Figure 14-A

I will be watching the data closely and hope you will join in comparing the actual to the forecast. When you go to evaluate these forecasts, remember that tax policy does not predict the year-to-year fluctuations, or when recessions come, but a period of a few years that is predicted to be stronger than another period *should* be stronger.

I assume brackets will be adjusted for inflation, but that the top bracket will decline 0.05 GDP/p each year, since historically GDP/p grows faster than inflation.

In the figures below the black lines show what we are making predictions of: growth, trade or the share to employees. The model's estimates shown in thick lighter gray lines are based on actual tax policy with current policy continuing and that beginning in 2018 the effect is as though the top rate were 34 percent. The darker thinner gray lines show the estimates based on a top rate of 37 percent and 29.6 percent.

GDP

First we will look at economic growth. We'll use two models: the one from Chapter 3, which fits data from all three variables since 1920, and the one from Chapter 13, which fits data since 1984 using the two tax rates. Since 1984 the top bracket has been consistently below 10 GDP/p and has played a limited role in growth.

Both models show growth improving in 2018. The model in Figure 14-B (fitted to data since 1920) estimates 2.6 percent growth while the one in 14-C (fitted to more recent data) shows 3.3 percent growth in 2018.

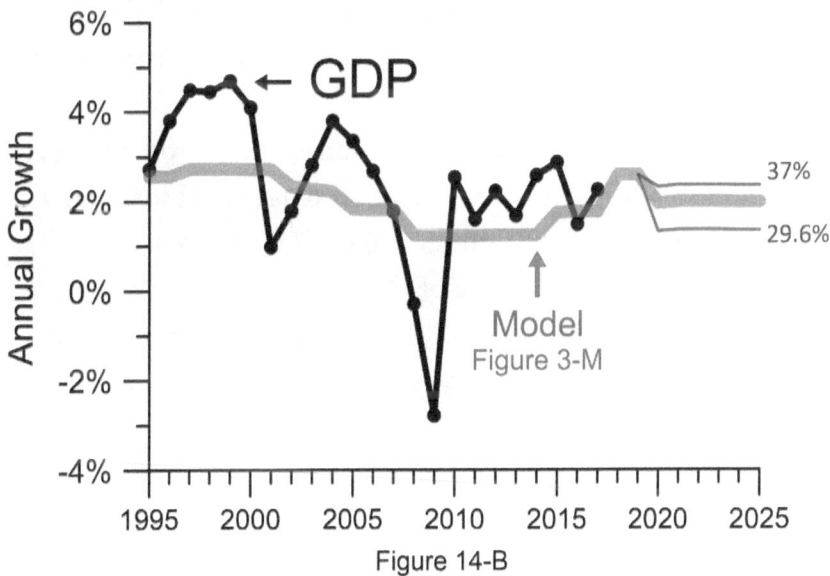

Figure 14-B

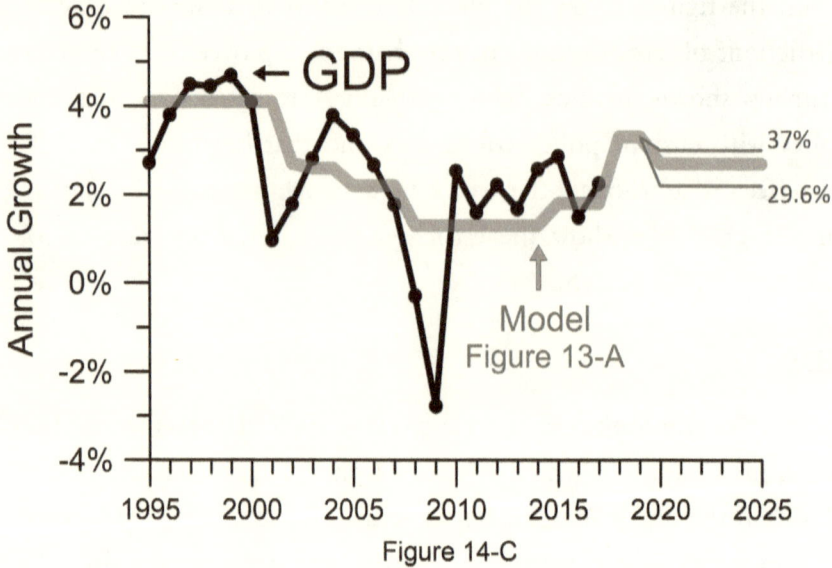

Figure 14-C

Complicating these growth estimates is that the economy will almost certainly go into recession sometime in the next three years. The current expansion is already the second longest on record. Consumer credit and corporate debt have risen to levels that in the past proved to be excessive and corresponded with recessions.

If the underlying growth rate for 2018 and 2019 is 3.3 percent as the second model suggests and we get a recession in 2018 growth might bounce back to 4 or even 5 percent in 2019.

It's possible when the 2020 election comes Trump will have had the strongest year of GDP growth since 2000. He could look like an economic genius compared to Bush (43) and Obama. While I would be crediting the lagged influence of the higher capital-gains rate put in place by Obama, Republicans and the financial media would likely lavish praise on Republicans, tax-cuts, and deregulation.

On the other hand, seven of the last eight years grew faster than the estimated growth of the models. Perhaps the next three years will all grow below the forecasted rate. If a recession started in 2020 it would strain Trump's reelection effort. All the Republican

Presidents who won reelection in the last ninety years had a recession their first year in office and a robust economy as they campaigned for reelection.

There could be enough strength in the economy for a Trump 2020 campaign victory. However, a better measure of Trump's impact on the economy will begin in 2020 after the two year lag of the 2018 tax cut. Growth from 2020 through the third quarter of 2024 will give voters in 2024 the clearest picture of economic performance under Trump.

Wages

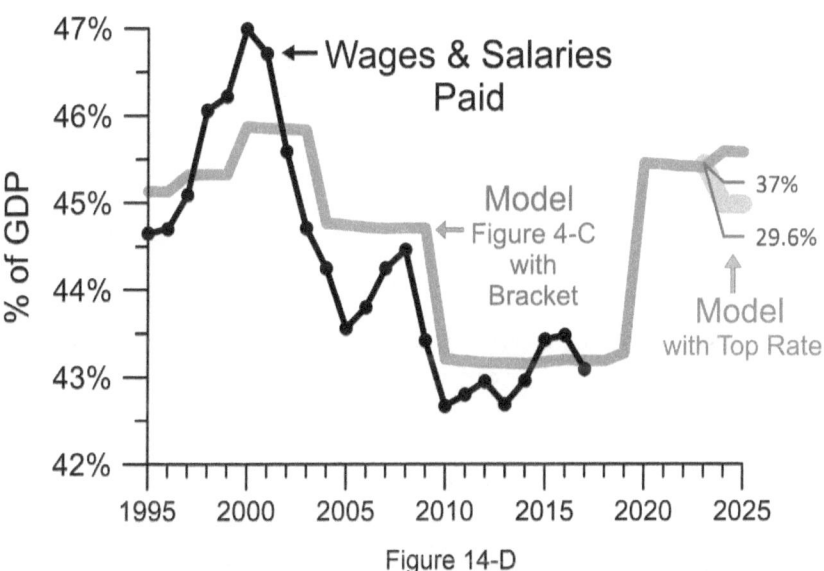

Figure 14-D

The model estimates a huge bounce in employee compensation in time to influence the 2020 election. The 45.5 percent of GDP estimate would be labor's highest share since 2002. Unless there's a recession, the working class could view Trump as their triumphant hero and propel him to a 2020 election victory. Ironically the capital gains tax increase under Obama propels the jump in the estimate similar to how Reagan helped growth under Clinton.

If part of the corporate tax burden is actually bourn by workers as we have speculated earlier in this book labor's share could go even higher due to the corporate tax rate cut.

Trumps tax cut should start affecting workers share of the pie in 2024. Raising the top bracket to $600,000 should help workers. A model using the top rate instead of the top bracket shown for the years 2023 through 2025 in Figure 14-D suggests the cut to the top rate will harm workers starting in 2024.

Usually a tax change moves the top rate and bracket in the same direction rather than in opposite directions. The top bracket making the top rate statistically insignificant in the model likely means the level of the top bracket historically includes much of the influence of the top rate paired with it. Since rate and bracket moved in opposite directions the result starting in 2024 could be different and should be watched closely.

Balance of Trade

The trade-balance should improve in 2018 toward the model's estimate of minus-1.8 percent of GDP. The next recession when it comes should improve the deficit to at least that level. After 2019 the Trump pass-through tax rate should have the trade deficit fluctuating around the minus-2.3 percent estimate.

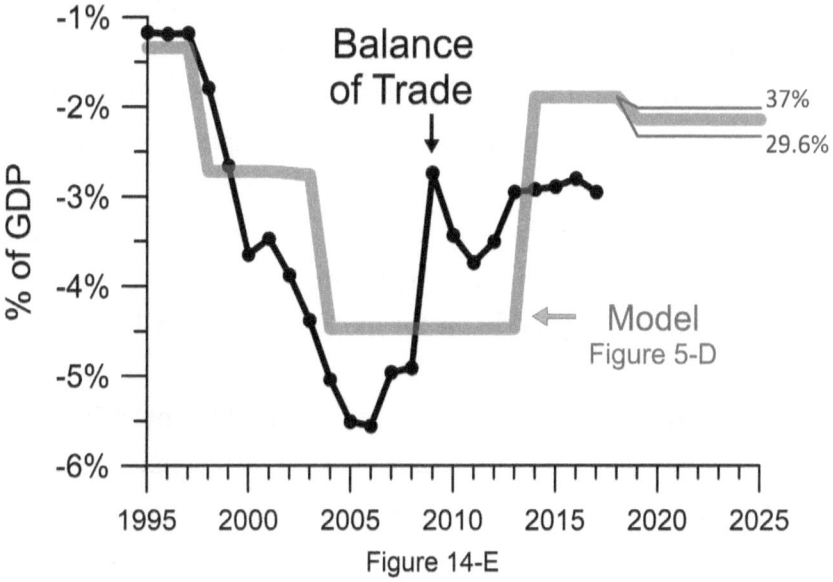

Figure 14-E

Learning the Lesson

Restoring prosperity requires voters learn when tax policy affects the economy as well as how. If we don't learn that we remain the pawns of politicians and the media who spin the data as it comes out to support any agenda they choose.

President Trump's tax cut should start influencing the trade deficit in 2019, GDP growth in 2020 and labors share of the pie in 2024.

The model's above suggest the capital gains tax rate going up in 2013 should improve the trade deficit and labor's share of the pie during President Trump's watch. While it would be normal and expected for Trump to take credit the nation is better served when voters have a clearer picture of reality.

If the tax cut remains in place through 2022 it will influence GDP growth from 2020 through 2024. If growth during this period is weak let's not make the mistake of the Great Depression and blame Republicans rather than bad tax policy. In 2024 people who are fifty-five or older will have seen three times in their adult lives that tax-cuts temporally coincided with strength, but were followed by weakness. Weakness followed cutting the top rate to 28 percent in 1988 and also after cutting the top rate and capital-gains rate in 2003.

Sometimes we can learn from making a mistake one time. Some lessons take making the mistake hundreds of times. If this book helps the third time be the charm for our generation, I will count it a success.

If Democrats take control of Washington in 2018 or 2020 and then the weak growth follows let's not blame them, but keep the focus on the tax policy that can restore prosperity.

Fixing the problem will require higher marginal tax rates and brackets. Perhaps we have begun to turn the corner toward better tax policy. Trump's tax cut should not be as destructive to growth as the Bush tax cuts and not nearly as bad as the cuts preceding the Great Depression.

Trump did not eliminate the capital gains tax rate or take it down to the 15 percent or 12.5 percent that corresponded with the great recession and Great Depression. His pass-through tax rate which could in effect give elite business owners a 29.6 percent tax rate on money pulled out of businesses comes with requirements for having real capital and compensating employees. Even with the full discount it is not as bad as the 28 percent top rate corresponding with the 1990 recession or 25 percent rate of the depression.

Trump will probably face a recession and huge budget deficits before he has a chance to run for reelection. I see no reason he could not play the role of hero (as Hoover, Reagan, and Bush [41] did) and raise marginal rates and brackets at the top of the income tax schedule, especially if he cares about budget deficits and the working-class base that helped elect him.

Electing officials who will fix the problem with higher tax brackets would initially be harder on Republicans, unless Republican primary voters radically change their view on taxes. Republicans could play a vital role in making sure tax brackets are high enough on high marginal tax rates.

In this chapter we saw how growth in the economy and workers share of the pie might favor Trump's reelection in 2020. We looked at future implications of Trump's tax-cuts. Going into the 2024 election we will know the growth rate for the four and three quarter year period from 2020 through the third quarter of 2024. If this growth rate is below 3 percent and especially if it is in the low 2 percent range or worse, every voter in 2024 should recognize that low marginal tax rates on high personal income is a failed policy.

In the next and final chapter, we will see the current concentrations of income, wealth, and power in excess of the beneficial level are nothing new—the acrimony, weakness, and problems that accompany this over-concentration have occurred many times. The wealthy winning at class-warfare is part of a long cycle repeated throughout history. We are in the crisis phase of that cycle . . .

Which also means there's great opportunity.

Chapter 15
Crisis is Opportunity

Success consists of going from failure to failure without a loss of enthusiasm. —Winston Churchill

Perspective defines whether one's circumstances are a problem or an opportunity. Individually and collectively, pain, hardship, and crisis present great opportunities, disguised and hard to see as they usually are. Whatever pain we experienced in the last ten years—and may experience in the next eight—presents the opportunity to make the twenty-first century another *American* century.

When I was going through the pain of separation and divorce, I thought about the fifteen or twenty things I had been most upset about during the marriage. It became clear they all had a common denominator of disrespect.

Then the still voice inside said, "And it's your own fault. You didn't respect yourself."

In the eternal scheme of things, perhaps the world's role is to reflect back to us the issues where we need growth. Ideally, the spiritual maturity needed for a happy marriage would have emerged during or before the marriage, but spiritual growth didn't come until our suffering made clear the need for it.

It is when we are challenged and push beyond or are forced out of a comfort zone that growth comes. Sometimes you will hear a successful business owner say something like, "The best thing that ever happened to me was getting fired." When things go contrary to our hopes, we tend to ponder and grow more than we would during pleasant and easy circumstances.

When the national economy dips down, businesses less adapt at meeting the needs of people fail. Resources and labor are freed up and entrepreneurs can redeploy them more productively in the next upturn. Usually the strongest rate of growth in a business cycle comes within a year or two after a recession. The best ten-year period of U.S. growth ever—annualizing 10.3 percent—followed the worst seven-year period ever.

The Heartbeat of History

The Great Depression was more than just a business cycle—it was part of a longer cycle. It was one precedent of many for the current concentration of wealth, power, and income at the top. Will and Ariel Durant, who wrote eleven volumes of *The Story of Civilization*, write in their summary book entitled *The Lessons of History*, "The concentration of wealth is natural and inevitable, and is periodically alleviated by violent or peaceable partial redistribution. In this view all economic history is the slow heartbeat of the social organism, a vast systole and diastole of concentrating wealth and compulsive recirculation" (p. 57).

William Strauss and Neil Howe, who wrote *The Fourth Turning*, believe what the Durants call a heartbeat is an eighty- to one-hundred-year cycle with four turns or phases. In the third turn, wealth becomes concentrated; in the fourth turn, a crisis climaxes with a revolution, either political or violent, that disperses wealth somewhat.

By their account, the "fourth turns" in America are the Revolutionary War, the Civil War, and the combination of the Great Depression and World War II. In the 1990s they predicted the next fourth turn would begin around 2005 and climax by 2025.

Earlier I mentioned I sometimes calculate changes over thirty-six-year periods. The thirty-six-year growth rate shown in Figure 15-A supports the idea of an eighty- to hundred-year cycle. The cycle bottomed in 1934 and should bottom again around 2025, or perhaps later.

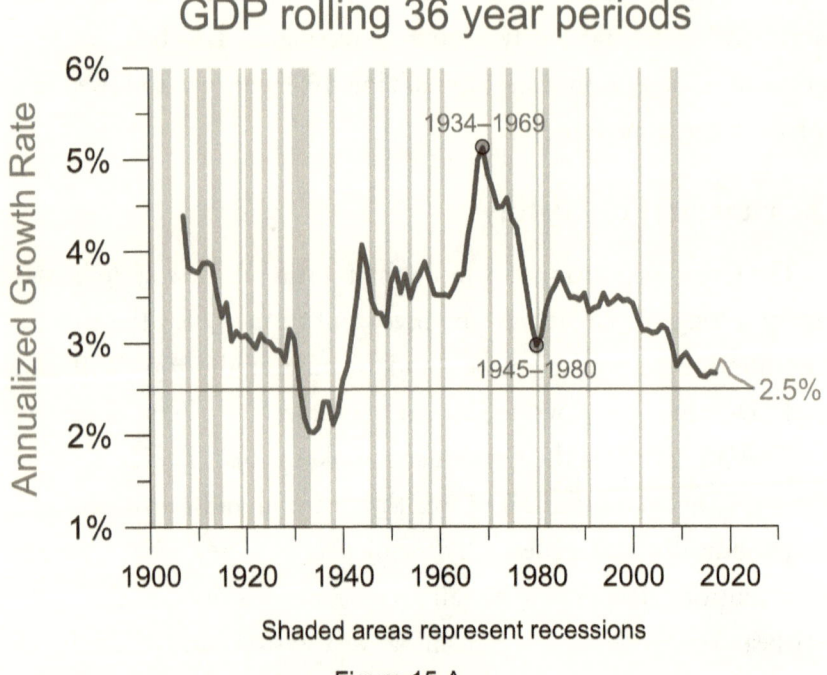

Figure 15-A

Our hero Hoover launched the all time best thirty-six year period with his big tax increase, 1934–1969 grew at 5.1 percent. The average top tax rate for the period was 83.7 percent with a top bracket averaging 1438 GDP/p.

FDR launched the weakest period between the Great Depression and great recession by trying to soak the rich, 1945–1980 grew at 3.0 percent. The top rate and bracket averaged 80.9 percent and 99.7 GDP/p.

As bad as trying to soak the rich can be, coddling them with low marginal tax rates is worse. We tried it in the Great Depression and with the 1986 tax reform. That reform took the top rate down to 28 percent in 1988 which with the two year lag began influencing growth in 1990.

I'm estimating the 1990–2025 period will grow at 2.5 percent, so far 1990–2017 has grown at 2.4 percent. The top marginal rate faced by business owners for the whole period will likely average 35.3 percent with a top bracket averaging 8.0 GDP/p.

The thirty-six year rate should improve in 2018 as the 1981-82 recession drops out of the period. Then the strong growth influenced by Reagan's 50 percent top rate rolls out and is replaced with growth influenced by Trump's tax cut.

Let these two facts sink in before you vote again: the best period ever started with a high top rate and bracket. Tax reform with the lowest average top tax rate since the Depression and the lowest average brackets ever will likely prove to be the worst policy since the Great Depression.

If Strauss and Howe's theory is correct and the economy goes as I expect, the 2024 election could be the climax of the crisis/revolution.

And we thought the *2016* election was big.

Strauss and Howe theorize that generations coming of age in each "turn" have distinct characteristics. The generation coming of age during the crisis is a "hero" generation. They are more civic-minded and tend to be less self-serving. Some call the last "hero" generation, which came of age during the Great Depression, the "greatest generation."

The greatest generation built institutions that enabled renewal, progress, and prosperity, but not just in America. They made international institutions instrumental to a majority of nations becoming democratic for the first time in history.

My generation, the baby boomers, who came of age in great prosperity, Strauss and Howe call a "prophet generation." Our role is to tear down all the institutions we believe are not working. Strauss and Howe predicted we would create lots of acrimony and divisiveness. They may have us pegged.

If we get the expected weak growth from 2020 through 2025 the baby boomers might experience enough pain to collectively change our view about taxes and fulfill the role of tearing down the institutions that don't work. This could include changing the leadership of, or defunding, every institution, foundation, think-tank and political group that supports low marginal tax rates at high levels of personal income.

Yet we are only part of the cycle, and as a recession in the business cycle creates space for entrepreneurs to grow great business from the ashes of failed ones, so a fourth turn enables the next hero generation to create new institutions that carry the country—and perhaps all of civilization—to new heights.

Millennials are coming of age in a crisis. They are our next hero generation. The 2015 Millennial Impact Report conducted by the consulting firm Achieve found 84 percent of millennials made charitable contributions, but they are less likely to contribute the way their parents did and less likely to support causes at work picked by the head of their company. Millennials are diverse and not all studies conclude they are more civic minded. Let us hope their noble side comes forth.

Mark Zuckerberg, one of the most famous millennials, has set a goal of connecting the whole world into a community; he views this as his purpose, or at least *one* of his purposes. When he started Facebook, he thought someone should connect the world. He didn't think he might be the one to do it until years later.

In a 2017 address to Harvard graduates, Zuckerberg urged them to build a community which would encourage and enable everyone to pursue a purpose that benefits the world. He said starting

Facebook was possible in part because he knew that if he failed he had a safety net of family that would keep him from disaster and enable him to advance some other purpose. He envisions a community that provides everyone a safe space in order to fulfill a purpose.

Listening to Zuckerberg's speech (shared on Facebook, of course) reminded me of how Strauss and Howe say a nation emerges stronger from a fourth-turn crisis when society tires of divisiveness and longs more for community. While emerging stronger may be more common, a nation can also fail. They note that the Roman Empire went through twelve of the long cycles before failing.

Leading up to the fourth turn of Rome's last cycle, the wealthy had the political power to pay almost no taxes. There was not enough money to fund the legions in the field. Word was sent, saying, "We can't afford to pay your wages, but do the best you can." The Roman Legions mostly dissolved and the barbarians advanced to the gates of the city of Rome, having faced little Roman military opposition. The Dark Ages began with sacking the city of Rome.

Greed left to its own devices kills. It can kill countries, companies, individuals, and the goose that lays the golden eggs. Yet greed can be channeled by appropriate law, regulation, and tax policy to serve the public good. Good government is a major part of Adam Smith's "invisible hand" (mentioned in Chapter 1), which aligns self-interest with the public good.

When incentives are right, markets enable amazing progress and prosperity that lifts everyone. When incentives are wrong, vast potential is left on the table; those in power tend to exploit and ignore the rest while frustration builds.

This was the case in 594 BC when Solon was elected as Archon of Athens and given near-dictatorial powers to prevent revolution.

The Durants tell the story in *The Life of Greece* based on Plutarch's account. Conditions had worsened each year for the poor, and corrupt courts ruled against them at every turn. There was talk of violent revolt, while the rich prepared to protect themselves and their property by force.

Upon taking office, Solon devalued the currency, thus easing the burden on debtors—this was at his personal expense as he was a large creditor; he ended imprisonment for debt; he reorganized the courts to be fairer for all; for any Athenian killed in battle, he provided education for their children at government expense.

He adopted a progressive income tax that taxed the rich at twelve times the rate of the poor. The rich complained his policies were outright confiscation. Radicals complained he wasn't solving the problem because he did not redistribute the land.

A generation later, almost everyone credited him with restoring prosperity and saving Athens from violent revolution.

About a century after the reforms of Solon, the Persian Empire invaded Greece, intending to crush the city-state of Athens. Athenians routed the vastly larger Persian army on the plains of Marathon. Would Athenians have fought so valiantly, if they didn't value their own way of life? Outcomes tend to be better when everyone believes they have a place in society worth protecting.

We Are All In This Together

We are all connected. One person's potential going undeveloped detracts from all of society. One person with the power to take more than they actually produce reduces the incentive of others to produce and raises the risk some feel their lot in life doesn't warrant protecting society—and may enable imagining violence is justified.

The tax policy that helps distribute incentive to best grow the economy will also give the most people a place in society worth protecting.

We are at the point of the Durants' "heartbeat of history," where the chamber is ready to contract and pump life-giving oxygenated blood into the social organism. Strauss and Howe say going from the fourth-turn crisis to a first turn in a new cycle of progress comes when people long more for community than they do to "prove" those they disagree with wrong.

The efficiency of the chamber's contraction or turn of the cycle in regenerating our lives depends on us. How will we vote? How will we treat each other? Will we be champions of progress or victims of circumstance?

When we blame someone for our problems who has a different view or a different interest, or we call them idiots or think of them as evil, we cast ourselves into the role of victim. As a victim, you sacrifice your power to help solve problems. It's like a NASCAR driver forgetting to watch the road and focusing on the wall instead.

If you don't want to hit the wall and crash, focus on the path forward. We tend to get what we focus on. When we blame and call names, we focus on the *problem*—and get more of it. If you pay attention to the cars spinning out of control, you fail to focus on the gap between the cars. Focus on the path forward.

When you blame or call names it says to the universe, "Oh, look at me! The poor, sympathy-deserving victim!" You not only give up most or all of your ability to move forward or avoid a crash, you also create resistance to any forward progress from those you blamed or labeled. It is not without reason Jesus taught calling someone a fool risks condemning yourself to hellfire (Matt. 5:22 KJV).

An attack on someone else is an attack on yourself and the nation.

Our political system has given up so much power and created so much resistance that almost nothing good can be accomplished.

The path forward between all the objects spinning out of control was spelled out in Chapter 13, but it bears repeating.

Forgive yourself and everyone else.

Recognize everyone is doing the best they know how.

They have probably heard of better, but if they actually knew better they would do it.

The pain of the kindergarten experience and of the divorce became a path forward when I chose to give up being a victim and forgive. Giving up victimhood and forgiveness go hand in hand on the path forward.

When you choose to move forward and treat everyone with respect under all circumstances you empower yourself, you lessen the resistance to your forward progress, and you set an example where others might actually learn to do better.

Everyone's choice matters, but the actions and words of our wealthiest and most influential have a bigger impact on prosperity or decline.

Some of our elites imagine they are victims of a progressive income tax. We need you to give up the role of victim and play the role of society's builder. We need you to build your wealth in the big tax-free pocket of a business that benefits others. We need you to tolerate, if not rejoice in, labor getting the share of the pie that best promotes prosperity. Recognize that higher marginal tax rates on you help create more sustainable wealth for all.

In chaotic systems, much like life, subtle variations in the beginning of a process can make massive differences at the end. As the saying goes, How a butterfly flaps its wings in one part of the world could be the difference of whether a hurricane hits another part.

Every time someone becomes familiar with the ideas of this book, or votes for progress or treats another with respect and kindness, it creates a ripple. The interactions of all the ripples make waves that unfold our future.

Politicians pay close attention to the margin of victory in races all over the country. Every vote matters. As Teel Bivins, the late Ambassador to Sweden and a State Senator from Amarillo for many years, once told me, "There are two ways to run for office—scared . . . and unopposed."

Politicians will carefully analyze the issues that drive the margins of victory in the 2018 election. Even if 2018 makes no immediate difference in tax policy, small changes in how people vote will be noticed and could become a massive wave by 2024.

You have made a long journey with me. You probably understand marginal tax rates better than almost anyone who has not read this book. Cutting marginal tax rates at the low end of the income spectrum likely benefits the incentive to work and grow. However, you have seen a strong case that marginal rates should be raised at the high end, with high-enough brackets to keep average tax rates low.

You have seen how the tax changes proposed in this book would encourage elites to grow their businesses more, or as we call it, put money in their big pocket. While elites would give up some consumption in the short term, in the long run they would make themselves and everyone else better off.

You have seen evidence that higher tax rates and brackets would shift more incentive to workers, and how this is tied to America's economic status in the world. You now can ponder that the budget and trade deficits mainly stem from bad tax policy.

You may need to see a few more years of data from this new perspective before you are convinced, but that's okay.

You have lived through some or all of the economic weakness these last twenty-eight years, along with the political bitterness, placed in the context of a long social cycle that has played out many times. Before 2025 you will likely see a recession or two, some years with massive budget deficits and perhaps an asset bubble decades in the making pop.

Whether we have great problems or great opportunities depends on our perspective.

In the next few years we will pass from the end of one cycle to the beginning of a new one. The outcome of the next hundred years will be subject to chaos theory: sensitive dependence on initial conditions.

How you vote and treat others in the next few years could define the quality of life for your children and grandchildren.

Vote for prosperity every chance you get.

Let us love ourselves and our neighbors and our children enough to focus on the path forward.

Urgent Plea!

Thank you for reading the book! What did you think? Your feedback is appreciated. I love hearing what you have to say.

Your feedback will make future additions better—and maybe the country, too.

Please leave me an honest REVIEW on Amazon. Or contact me directly at John@EconomicLeads.com

Thanks so much!

About the Author

John H. Early has been a registered investment advisor since 1991. He studied economics at Vanderbilt University. He has independently researched the economy and financial markets for over three decades. He published a paid-subscription economic newsletter in the 1980s and 1990s and is currently a contributor at SeekingAlpha.com.

www.ingramcontent.com/pod-product-compliance
Lightning Source LLC
Chambersburg PA
CBHW030624220526
45463CB00004B/1411